Red Power

THE NATIVE AMERICAN
CIVIL RIGHTS MOVEMENT

Red Power

THE NATIVE AMERICAN CIVIL RIGHTS MOVEMENT

TROY R. JOHNSON
Department Chair
American Indian Studies
California State University,
Long Beach

SERIES EDITOR: PAUL C. ROSIER
Assistant Professor of History
Villanova University

CHELSEA HOUSE
PUBLISHERS
An imprint of Infobase Publishing

RED POWER: The Native American Civil Rights Movement

Copyright © 2007 by Infobase Publishing

Chelsea House
An imprint of Infobase Publishing
132 West 31st Street
New York NY 10001

Library of Congress Cataloging-in-Publication Data
Johnson, Troy R.
Red power : the Native American civil rights movement / Troy R. Johnson.
    p. cm. — (Landmark events in Native American history)
Includes bibliographical references and index.
ISBN-13: 978-0-7910-9341-2 (hardcover)
ISBN-10: 0-7910-9341-7 (hardcover)
1. Indians of North America—Politics and government.   2. Indians of North America—Civil rights.   3. Indians of North America—Government relations.   4. American Indian Movement—History.   5. Wounded Knee Massacre, S.D., 1890.   6. Wounded Knee (S.D.) —History—Indian occupation, 1973.   7. Civil rights movements—United States.   8. United States—Race relations.   9. United States—Politics and government.   I. Title.
E98.T77J65 2007
323.1197'073—dc22   2006102264

Series design by Erika K. Arroyo
Cover design by Ben Peterson

Printed in the United States of America

Bang NMSG 10 9 8 7 6 5 4 3 2 1

This book is printed on acid-free paper.

Contents

Introduction to the Red Power Movement

THE 1973 OCCUPATION OF WOUNDED KNEE, SOUTH Dakota, took place in the midst of a national backlash against the war in Vietnam, the rise of the Black Power and La Raza movements in the United States, and followed on the heels of the 19-month American Indian occupation of Alcatraz Island, from December 1969 to July 1971. Whereas the occupation of Alcatraz Island had been carried out by a nonconfrontational group of San Francisco Bay Area Indian college students— Indians of All Tribes—the occupation of Wounded Knee would be carried out by a new, more militant group on the national activist scene: the American Indian Movement, better known as AIM.

The American Indian Movement was founded in 1968 by Clyde Bellecourt, Eddie Benton Banai, Dennis Banks, and Mary Jane Wilson, all four Chippewa Indians from Minnesota. AIM arose out of concerns of Native Americans in Minneapolis, Minnesota, and focused on changing the lives of Indians in urban centers.

The American Indian Movement (AIM) was founded in 1968 by Clyde Bellecourt, Eddie Benton Banai, Dennis Banks, and Mary Jane Wilson. Bellecourt (left) is pictured here with fellow AIM leader Russell Means in Minneapolis, Minnesota, in 1973.

AIM members coordinated a neighborhood patrol to monitor police activities in Indian neighborhoods and to prevent unjust arrests and police mistreatment of American Indian residents. The Minneapolis police often waited outside of bars frequented by Indian people, and at closing time they would confront them. Indian people claimed that they were beaten, the women sexually assaulted, and then thrown into jail without cause. AIM ultimately extended its area of concern to include the reform of Indian and federal government relations. AIM attracted a whole new generation of Indian youth and carried out the 1970 occupation of South Dakota's Mount Rushmore, and the following year a symbolic Thanksgiving Day occupation of a replica of the *Mayflower* sailing ship at Plymouth Rock, in Massachusetts. Their "Trail of Broken Treaties" caravan to Washington, D.C., in 1972 concluded with the seven-day occupation of the federal Bureau

THE FOUNDING OF AIM

In 1966, Dennis Banks, an Anishinabe (Chippewa) Indian, was convicted of burglary and sentenced to prison in Stillwater State Penitentiary in Minnesota. While in prison, Banks met fellow convict and Anishinabe Clyde Bellecourt, who was also serving time at Stillwater for burglary. It was while in prison that they began to formulate the beginning of an organization that would address the problems that beset Indian people and find solutions to basic needs such as housing and employment. To help Native Americans live successfully beyond the boundaries of reservations, they would establish a series of survival schools in Minneapolis and St. Paul, Minnesota. Their primary focus was to restore pride to Native Americans and to preserve Indian culture. Along with Eddie Benton Banai and Mary Jane Wilson, they founded the American Indian Movement (AIM).

of Indian Affairs' headquarters. During that occupation, AIM members, seeking evidence of broken treaties and misuse of Indian trust money by the BIA, took vast numbers of confidential BIA and Indian Health Service (IHS) records and caused approximately $2 million in damage to BIA headquarters. Most notable among all their protest actions, however, was the 1973 occupation of the town of Wounded Knee, South Dakota, which lasted 71 days.

THE ROOTS OF AMERICAN INDIAN ACTIVISM

American Indian activism began long before the 1960s and 1970s. Its roots stretch back to the first encounter between European explorers and the indigenous peoples of Mesoamerica in 1492; between indigenous North Americans and the colonists of the Jamestown settlement in present-day Virginia after 1607; and in 1622, between the Indians of southern New England and the Puritans of the Massachusetts Bay and Plymouth colonies. The reasons for American Indian activism are complicated and simple at the same time: protection of homeland security and the recognition, by the invaders, of the national sovereignty of the peoples already present in the "New World."

The First Attack on Native Sovereignty

From 1636 to 1637, the Puritans attacked the Pequot Indians who were living in southern New England. Unlike the Mohicans and Narragansetts, the Pequots refused to cede their traditional lands to the Puritans. In 1634, a group of unidentified Indians killed an English slave hunter named John Stone and eight of his companions who were looking for Native American slaves. The Narragansetts were treaty partners with the Puritans and are now the ones believed to have actually committed the murders. However, the Puritans used Stone's death to claim jurisdiction over the Pequots and to demand the surrender of land, trade goods, and Stone's killers. The Pequots, hoping to avoid war, agreed to the Puritan demands but later failed to provide the required goods.

In 1636, several Narragansetts killed an English trader and sought sanctuary among the Pequots. When the Puritans demanded the surrender of the Narragansetts, the Pequots refused and a brief skirmish ensued. In May 1637, the Massachusetts General Court drew up articles of war, raised an army, and marched against the Pequots, surrounding their village and fort on the Mystic River. Puritans and Narragansetts set fire to the village, killing as many as 700 men, women, and children.

A New World?

In fact, the lands that the Europeans pillaged for profit did not represent a new world. Demographers estimate the Native American population in the area known as Mesoamerica (present-day Central America) to have been as high as 63 million people. In the area represented by the present-day United States, there were some 500 separate Native American nations with a total population of approximately 10 million. These nations spoke more than 300 languages and another 150 or so dialects. The people within the individual nations were not related to those of another nation by blood, kin, religion, culture, or tradition.

It is difficult to speak in sweeping generalizations regarding all Indian nations, but generally speaking, native peoples had no concept of land ownership as it is known today. What they did have, however, was a keen sense of territoriality. They knew where their lands were, and to cross the boundaries of another nation, to trespass, usually resulted in punishment or a demand for payment in trade goods such as furs, skins, or foodstuffs.

Indian people practiced a movement pattern known as the "seasonal round." They knew when food and game animals would be available in different parts of their established territory, and so they moved around to take advantage of the natural offerings provided by seasonal growth and game migration. They also were aware that weather patterns made life difficult in some areas at specific times of the year and pleasant in other areas at other times. This explains why many Native Americans moved about throughout the year. It is incorrect to state, as the Europeans did, that Indian peoples were nomadic, wandering without homes or settlements. These were a people with direction and purpose. This cultural misunderstanding would cause severe problems that sometimes led to warfare when Europeans saw land that they perceived to be vacant and free for the taking—when, in fact, the Indian owners of the land were in a different part of their territory due to the availability of natural resources.

Despite writings and films to the contrary, Native American societies were, by and large, sophisticated, with established forms of religion, government, trade, technology, and lifestyles. Europeans simply did not understand, or want to acknowledge, the existence of these attributes, because that would mean that these were settled people, not "savages." The recognition of settled societies would have meant that the Europeans would have had to recognize land ownership and the need to negotiate for lands in order to establish a foothold in North America. It was much simpler to deny the existence of sophisticated societies, classify the inhabitants as savages or devils of the forest, and take by force, without guilt or punishment. Such was the settlement of the United States.

It is from this traumatic pattern of European settlement that American Indian activism emerged. Contrary to the European example of simply taking by force, Native American nations first attempted to compromise with and assist these new arrivals to the continent. Indians fought alongside the British against the French in the French and Indian War and alongside the colonists against the British in the Revolutionary War. After the Revolutionary War and the founding of the United States, Indian peoples and nations used the newly established U.S. court system as a tool to preserve their way of life.

In other parts of America, the Spanish, with their priests and conquistadors, came to the "New World" in the quest for God, Glory, and Gold. They came to America for God in the sense that they attempted to convert any inhabitants they came in contact with to Catholicism. The Spanish were required to read a royal document to indigenous peoples prior to any violence taken against a Mesoamerican city or village. The Spanish Requirement of 1513, as it was called, was of course not

EARLY NATIVE AMERICAN SOCIETIES

Just one example of sophisticated Native American technology can be seen among the mound building societies of Ohio, Illinois, and Tennessee. From about 600 to 450 B.C., the people of the Adena, Hopewell, and Mississippian societies built massive geometric and animistic earthworks. The Adena people built the famed Serpent Mound with a body that measured more than 1,200 feet (380 meters) long. They also built other earthen mounds in the shapes of bears and eagles that were aligned geometrically with celestial bodies. The Hopewell society built earthen mounds, too, and was also known for participating in trade networks that extended from the Great Lakes to the Gulf of Mexico. The Natchez society in present-day Tennessee built huge step mounds similar to those found in present-day Central America. The base of their largest mound is bigger than the base of the largest pyramid in Egypt.

Europeans did not understand, or want to acknowledge, the existence of these attributes among Native American societies, because that would mean that these were settled societies, not groups of "savages." Unfortunately, through the mid-1800s, European settlers still held the notion that the mounds were constructed by a variety of people—Vikings, Greeks, the 10 Lost Tribes of Israel, even people from the Lost Continent of Atlantis—and not Native Americans.

read in the native peoples' language; furthermore, the document makes it clear that conversion was mandatory:

> If you do not do this, [convert to Catholicism] and maliciously make delay in it, I certify to you that, with the help of God, we shall powerfully enter into your country, and shall make war against you in all ways and manners that we can, and shall subject you to the yoke and obedience of the Church and of their highnesses; we shall take you, and your wives, and your children, and shall make slaves of them, and as such shall sell and dispose of them as their highnesses may command; and we shall take away your goods, and shall do you all the mischief and damage that we can, as to vassals who do not obey, and refuse to receive their lord, and resist and contradict him: and we protest that the deaths and losses which shall accrue from this are your fault, and not that of their highnesses, or ours, nor of these cavaliers who come with us.[1]

The Doctrine of Discovery and the Marshall Trilogy

This process of possession, coercion, and enslavement became known as the "Doctrine of Discovery," and, as can be seen above, failure to bow to the power of the Catholic Church made the consequences of the actions of the conquistadors, and later the settlers in the present-day United States, the fault of the native people. The 1823 U.S. Supreme Court decision in *Johnson v. McIntosh* incorporated the Doctrine of Discovery into U.S. law. Chief Justice John Marshall observed that European nations had forced Christianity on the inhabitants of America and that—"upon discovery"—the Indians had lost "their rights to complete sovereignty, as independent nations," and only retained a right of "occupancy in their lands." Marshall went on to state that the United States—upon declaring its independence in 1776—became a successor nation to the right of "discovery" and acquired the power of "dominion" from Great Britain.[2]

Johnson v. McIntosh was the first U.S. Supreme Court decision on the nature of Indian tribes' rights to land. The case actually involved a dispute between two white men: Thomas Johnson had obtained from an Indian tribe a deed to a certain plot of land, while William McIntosh had obtained a title to the same plot of land from the United States after the tribe had ceded the area by threat. Chief Justice John Marshall based the court's decision on a traditional understanding among European nations—that the discoverer of a territory had the exclusive right to purchase it from the native inhabitants. Therefore, Johnson lost his claim to the land. Interpreted more broadly, this case would later be used to overturn land cases in which individual U.S. states claimed to have purchased Indian lands. Only the federal government, represented by Congress, is allowed to terminate Indian land ownership.

Indian people, of course, did not see themselves as having been "discovered," nor did they believe that the United States had the right to claim their lands. In the next major Supreme Court decision pertaining to Native Americans, *Cherokee Nation v. Georgia*, Chief Justice Marshall clarified the nation status of Indian people when he stated that "Indian Nations are not sovereign nations in the same sense of Foreign Nations, but are more correctly denominated as domestic dependent nations."[3] Marshall went on to say that in the state of Georgia, the U.S. government now had a fiduciary responsibility toward Native American nations that could be compared to the relationship between a ward and his/her governor. Regarding land ownership, Chief Justice Marshall stated that Indian nations had a "possessory right" in land; that is to say that Indians could remain in possession of their land because they had possessed it since time immemorial. Indians could remain in possession of that land until such time as they relinquished the title to it, and that title could be passed only to the U.S. government, specifically to Congress. In its fiduciary relationship to Indian nations, only Congress could buy, sell, trade, or acquire Indian lands from Indian peoples or nations.

In the third case in what has been titled the Marshall Trilogy, *Worcester v. Georgia*, Chief Justice Marshall went even further. By unanimous consent, the U.S. Supreme Court ruled that Indian nations retained all the sovereign rights that they had prior to European discovery, unless those rights had been passed to Congress or had been taken in just war. These, Marshall stated, are "retained rights"—retained from time immemorial, not rights granted to Indian people by the U.S. government, and that these retained sovereign rights are not subject to regulation or interference by the individual states.[4] Marshall said that the individual states have no rights in "Indian country" even though that land might be within the physical boundaries of those individual states.

The Marshall Trilogy—*Johnson v. McIntosh, Cherokee Nation v. Georgia,* and *Worcester v. Georgia*—laid the groundwork for Indian activism. It is clear that Indian nations are nations (specifically, domestic dependent nations), that they have retained sovereignty, and that individual states have little or no authority over Indian people on their reservations. It is within this legal framework and these jurisdictional boundaries that American Indian activism comes to the forefront. The activism is about two issues primarily: that of encroachment on sovereignty and encroachment by the individual states onto Indian lands or into Indian issues.

2

Wounded Knee Creek: 1890

THE SELECTION OF THE VILLAGE OF WOUNDED KNEE AS A protest occupation site in 1973 had great historical and symbolic value for American Indian people, particularly the Lakota Sioux. At this same site on December 29, 1890, the 7th U.S. Cavalry massacred Sioux chief Big Foot and 300 of his followers. (The original 7th Cavalry had been decimated at the Battle of the Little Bighorn in 1876, when Lieutenant Colonel George Armstrong Custer, in an attempt to rebuild his tarnished reputation, led his men in an ill-advised attack; the entire group was wiped out by a much larger Indian force.) The victims were mostly women and children, their bodies left in the winter sleet and snow to freeze. Black Elk, a Lakota holy man and witness to the massacre as a young boy, later recalled:

> I did not know then how much was ended. When I look back now from this high hill of my old age, I can still see the butchered women and children lying heaped and scattered all along the crooked gulch as plain as when I saw

them with eyes still young. And I can see that something else died there in the bloody mud, and was buried in the blizzard. A people's dream died there. It was a beautiful dream. And I, to whom so great a vision was given in my youth—you see me now a pitiful old man who has done nothing, for the nation's hoop is broken and scattered. There is no center any longer, and the sacred tree is dead.[5]

THE GHOST DANCE

The link between the 1890 Wounded Knee massacre and the 1973 occupation of Wounded Knee is strong. The massacre occurred because of a fear by the U.S. Army that American Indian people, who had been confined to squalid Indian reservations, were preparing once again to go to war in protest of the continuing loss of land and the enormous loss of Indian lives to disease and warfare.

The army's fear grew out of the practice of a revitalization movement known as the Ghost Dance religion. The dance had been introduced by a Paiute Indian prophet named Wovoka. He was born around 1856 near Walker Lake in present-day Esmeralda County, Nevada. He grew up in the area of Mason Valley, Nevada, near today's Walker Lake Reservation, and was the son of Tavibo, a shaman whose visions prophesizing the demise of white people formed the basis for the Ghost Dance religion. Wovoka, whose name means "the Cutter" in Paiute, later took the name of his paternal grandfather, Kowhitgsaug. Upon the death of his father, Wovoka was taken into the family of a white farmer named David Wilson and was given the name Jack Wilson, by which he was known among local American settlers.

Wovoka's great revelation to his people occurred on January 1, 1889, during an eclipse of the sun, or a time "when the sun died." In December 1888, Wovoka had become ill with a severe fever. While in a feverish state, he received a vision, heard a "great noise," and then lost consciousness.

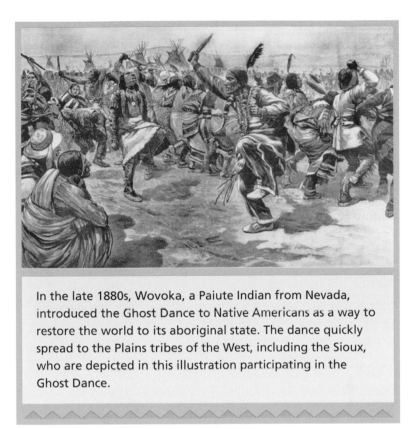

In the late 1880s, Wovoka, a Paiute Indian from Nevada, introduced the Ghost Dance to Native Americans as a way to restore the world to its aboriginal state. The dance quickly spread to the Plains tribes of the West, including the Sioux, who are depicted in this illustration participating in the Ghost Dance.

When he revived, he announced that he had been taken to the other world, where he had seen the Creator and all of the Indian people who had died in the past. The old had been made young again. Everyone was well fed, dancing, and blissfully happy. The Creator instructed Wovoka to return to the earth and tell the people that they must be good and love one another. Indian people were to cooperate with the white people and live in peace, without warfare, until the time when the Creator would remove all white people from the earth. Indian people were to abstain from drinking alcohol and were instructed not to fight, steal, or lie. They were instructed to work hard during their daily lives and pray for an apocalypse that would restore the world to its aboriginal state.

While in the presence of the Creator, Wovoka was given a number of powers, which included five songs for controlling the weather, maintaining peace and political responsibility, and prophesying. He was also given a sacred dance that he was to teach to his people. The dance was known to the Northern Paiute as *nanigukwa*, or "dance in a circle." Prior to the dance, the people were to prepare a feast that would feed everyone. The dance was to be performed for four successive nights, and on the last night they were to continue dancing until the morning of the fifth day. At that time they all were to bathe in the river and then disperse to their homes. The people were instructed to dance every six weeks. If the people obeyed these instructions, they would be reunited with family and friends in the other world, where there would be no sickness, old age, or death.

Wovoka's vision became the basis of the Ghost Dance religion, which was centered around the belief that there would be a time when all Indian people—the living and the dead—would be reunited on an earth that was spiritually regenerated and forever free from death, disease, and all the other miseries that had recently been experienced by Indian people. Word of the new religion spread quickly among the tribes of the Great Basin and Plains regions. Indian people representing more than 30 tribes traveled great distances to visit Wovoka and to learn more of his teachings, often returning home filled with messages of hope for their people. Many Indian people and tribes that had been devastated by war, reservation life, poverty, and disease, and who had undergone severe cultural and physical attacks, eagerly accepted the teachings of Wovoka. The U.S. Army's scorched-earth military policy instituted by generals William Tecumseh Sherman and Philip Sheridan, the destruction of the buffalo, confinement on reservations, and epidemics of strange and lethal diseases set the stage for the acceptance of Wovoka's message of revitalization.

As the religious movement spread, it took on features unique to individual tribes. Among the Lakotas, Wovoka's admonitions of peace were forgotten. Indian warriors and leaders such as Short Bull and Kicking Bear turned the prophet's teachings into a movement advocating violence against the white man. Soon the practice of the Ghost Dance included the introduction of a Ghost Dance shirt to the religion. The Ghost Dance shirt, it was believed, would protect the wearer and repel the white man's bullets. Non-Indians became alarmed by reports of what they believed to be Indian warriors performing this new war dance that was supposed to result in the disappearance of whites and the return of the buffalo. The wearing of the Ghost Dance shirt thus transformed Wovoka's religious movement into a warrior movement, in the minds of whites.

Government agents and missionaries opposed the Ghost Dance, and in 1890, the U.S. Army outlawed the Ghost Dance on Indian reservations. Tensions grew stronger between the Lakotas and the soldiers as Indian people left the reservations without permission to hunt and to participate in the Ghost Dance ritual out of sight of the army. Sitting Bull, a highly respected Lakota spiritual leader, was blamed for the unrest even though he was not a Ghost Dance leader. He was killed by Indian police in December 1890, when it was believed that he intended to join the Ghost Dancers who had left the Standing Rock Reservation in present-day South Dakota and North Dakota.

BIG FOOT AND WOUNDED KNEE CREEK

The U.S. Army was by this time concerned about the number of Indian men, women, and children who were leaving the Cheyenne River, Pine Ridge, and Standing Rock reservations to practice the new dance. It was feared that the Indian wars, which had so recently come to an end, were about to begin anew. In addition to Sitting Bull, who had been killed earlier that month, a young army captain reported that another prominent chief of the Miniconjou Sioux (a subtribe of the Lakota), Big Foot, was en route with some 300 warriors to join the Ghost Dancers. In fact, Big Foot was heading to the Pine Ridge Reservation to encourage the Indian people to return to their reservations. Fearing that he would possibly be arrested or punished by the U.S. government, Big Foot had accepted an offer from Chief Red Cloud to join him and his band on the Pine Ridge Reservation and to help in negotiating a peace before any warfare began. Red Cloud had been invited to the Pine Ridge Reservation to ensure that warfare did not break out between the U.S. Cavalry and the Indians who had left the reservations.

At the time, Big Foot was sick with pneumonia, and on December 28, 1890, had only reached Porcupine Butte when he and his followers were intercepted by Major Samuel Whiteside and the recently reconstructed 7th U.S. Cavalry. Of the 365 Indian persons arrested by Whiteside, only 116 were men. The men were poorly armed and represented no threat to the soldiers. Under orders from General John Brooke, Whiteside had Big Foot and his followers escorted to Wounded Knee Creek in present-day western South Dakota. Later that day, Colonel James Forsyth arrived and assumed command of the 7th Cavalry and Big Foot's Miniconjou encampment.

Upon arrival at Wounded Knee Creek, Big Foot and his followers were instructed to camp in an area that had been prepared by the U.S. Army. Whiteside demanded that Big Foot and his warriors turn over 25 rifles that he believed had been taken from the bodies of Custer's men following the Little Bighorn battle. Big Foot agreed to turn over the weapons, but a deadline was not established for the surrender of them. He posted a white peace flag over his tepee, and he and his followers settled down for a restless, cold night. Wasee Maza, one of the Indian survivors of the massacre, later

In late December 1890, Chief Big Foot of the Miniconjou Sioux attempted to lead more than 300 of his people to the Pine Ridge Reservation in present-day South Dakota when he was intercepted by Major Samuel Whiteside and the 7th U.S. Cavalry. Once he reached Pine Ridge, Big Foot planned to negotiate a peace treaty with the U.S. Army.

recalled, "There was a great uneasiness among the Indian all night because they were fearful that they were to be killed."[6]

Forsyth was unsure of the ability of his troops to disarm Big Foot and his followers, so he called for reinforcements. The new troops arrived during the night of December 28 and joined with the soldiers of the 7th Cavalry encamped on a small hill northwest of the Indian camp. Hotchkiss cannons were positioned on the hill, aimed at the Indian encampment.

The morning of December 29 dawned clear and cold on the Dakota plains. A hint of snowfall was in the wind. Forsyth was focused on disarming the Indians as quickly as possible and incarcerating them at the U.S. Army post at Gordon, Nebraska. He planned to have the warriors separated from the women and children and transferred by train to army headquarters in Omaha, Nebraska, where they would remain until the Ghost Dance threat was put down.

That morning, Forsyth ordered Big Foot and his followers to surrender all of their weapons. A group of Indian men brought a small cache of old rifles from the tepees and stacked them in front of the soldiers. None of the weapons were new enough to have come from the Custer battlefield. The soldiers, intent on finding the Custer rifles, went into the tepees and searched through bedding, clothing, and sacred bundles, but no additional weapons were found. Black Coyote, a Lakota holy man, then came forward holding a rifle in his hands. Wasee Maza tells the remainder of the story:

> The struggle for the gun was short, the muzzle pointed upward toward the east and the gun discharged. In an instant a volley followed and the people began falling.... [T]he soldiers were firing on Indians and stepping backwards and firing.... Right on the edge of the ravine on the south side were soldiers shooting at the Indians who were running down into the ravine, the soldiers' shots sounded like fire crackers and hail in a storm; a great many Indians

were killed and wounded down there. . . . When I went to the bottom of the ravine, [I] saw many little children lying dead in the ravine. . . . [W]hen I saw all those little infants lying there dead in their blood, my feeling was that even if I ate one of the soldiers, it would not appease my anger . . . While I was lying on my back, I looked down the ravine and saw these women, girls and little girls and boys coming up, I saw soldiers on both sides of the ravine shoot at them until they had killed every one of them. . . . I saw a young woman among them coming and crying and calling, "Mother! Mother!" She was wounded under her chin, close to her throat, and the bullet had passed through a braid of her hair and carried some of it into the wound, and then the bullet had entered from the front side of the shoulder and passed out the back side. Her Mother had been shot behind her. I got myself up and followed up the ravine. I saw many dead men, women, and children lying in the ravine.[7]

The firing at the Indian encampment lasted only about 10 minutes, while the firing at the ravine lasted for about an hour and a half. Most of the Indian warriors died in the initial onslaught, while many Indian women and children were killed by the Hotchkiss cannons firing into the ravine. By the time the shooting ended, the slight snowfall had turned into a blizzard and the 7th Cavalry left the dead and injured on the battlefield to freeze and to die. On January 3, 1891, a civilian burial party was escorted to Wounded Knee and 146 dead and frozen bodies were taken from the snow, loaded onto wagons, and buried in a mass grave near the church where the Hotchkiss cannons were positioned.

The total number killed at Wounded Knee Creek will never be known. Indian estimates of the massacre run from 250 to 300. There were few survivors. The Holy Cross Episcopal Church at Pine Ridge, decorated for Christmas, served as a makeshift hospital for 36 wounded Indians. A Christmas

After most of the members of Chief Big Foot's band were killed during the massacre at Wounded Knee Creek, South Dakota, on December 29, 1890, the Ghost Dance movement largely dissipated. Pictured here are 11 of the survivors of Big Foot's band of Miniconjou Sioux, a little more than a year after Wounded Knee.

tree was removed from the church, but green wreaths still decorated its windows and doors. The church pews were moved aside and armfuls of hay brought in upon which to lay the survivors. Young girls and women, babies and little children, and a few men, were treated. Brigadier General Leonard W. Colby was moved by the sight of one small Indian baby whose mother and father were believed to have been killed in the fighting. Colby took the child to his home in Beatrice, Nebraska, and named her Margaret Elizabeth. Colby learned later that the child's mother, Rock Bird, had survived the massacre and had named the girl Lost Bird. The fate of Lost Bird's father was never known. Colby met with Rock Bird and asked to be allowed to legally adopt the child. She initially objected to the adoption, but upon payment of $50, an agreement was reached. After the adoption, Lost Bird was raised by her white family but spent much of her adult life searching for her biological parents in South Dakota. She died in California in 1920.

3

Failed Indian Policy and the Birth of Red Power

SHORTLY BEFORE THE WOUNDED KNEE MASSACRE IN 1890, the U.S. government instituted a new Indian policy, which came in the form of the General Allotment Act (known as the Dawes Act). Under the terms of this law, which granted Indians U.S. citizenship, reservation land (in the form of allotments) was to be distributed among individual men, typically 160 acres for a head of household and 80 acres for an adult male. Unfortunately, the Dawes Act failed miserably—Native Americans' social structure was weakened, many were swindled out of their land, and the U.S. government mismanaged the reservations. Due to the failure of the Dawes Act, the U.S. government attempted to become less hands-on with the passage of the Indian Reorganization Act (IRA) in 1934. Under this law, the U.S. government promoted the establishment of written constitutions and charters that would allow tribes the ability to self-govern. The act terminated allotment, and surplus lands were returned to individual tribes. Unfortunately, to receive benefits from the IRA, tribes had to agree to the

U.S. government's terms, which meant creating a new tribal constitution and changing their existing political structure. In the end, more than one-third of the tribes voted against participating in the program; consequently, many no longer existed in the eyes of the U.S. government.

Due to decades of these failed policies and programs, the U.S. government instituted a new Indian policy in the 1940s and 1950s, which was influenced by an upswing in Americanization as a result of World War II. The federal government and white Americans favored a policy of assimilation of all people into mainstream U.S. society. Citizens not of European heritage were considered to be un-American. As a result, Native Americans who held on to their traditional cultural beliefs, especially those still living on Indian reservations, were targeted for conversion through government policies of assimilation and relocation. Treaties were abrogated, reservations abolished, and Indian people relocated into major urban areas—voluntarily if possible, but by force if necessary.

Thus, under President Dwight D. Eisenhower, the Bureau of Indian Affairs implemented the "relocation" and "termination" that would reinforce the Indian Reorganization Act. These two programs were designed to lure Indian people off the reservations and into major cities, such as San Francisco, in order to complete the assimilation and acculturation process. By the mid-1960s, the San Francisco Bay Area's urban Indian community was one of the largest and best organized in the country. Rather than dissolving into the urban "melting pot," Bay Area Indians tenaciously clung to their cultures, formed social and political organizations, and began to mobilize. Echoing the free speech, civil rights, and antiwar struggles and other social justice movements, Bay Area Indians began their own protest of Indian treaty and civil rights abuses. The Bay Area Indian movement, however, came within the framework of the larger Red Power movement, the development of which is described below.

THE RED POWER MOVEMENT IN CONTEXT

One of the first major protests among American Indians was carried out in the 1950s, when the people from the Six Nations of the Iroquois Confederacy (Cayuga, Mohawk, Oneida, Onondaga, Seneca, and Tuscarora) used passive resistance and militant protests to block various public works projects throughout New York State. Also during this period, Indians demonstrated in opposition to the building of power projects such as Fort Randall Dam on the Missouri River (in South Dakota) and Kinzua Dam on the border of Pennsylvania and New York. The construction of Kinzua Dam forced Pennsylvania's last Indian tribe, the Seneca, to relocate to New York.

In April 1958, Wallace P. "Mad Bear" Anderson (Tuscarora) led a stand against a tide of land seizures, a move that ultimately brought armed troops onto Indian land. The New York Power Authority planned to confiscate 1,383 acres of Tuscarora land for the building of a reservoir and the back flooding of Indian lands. Anderson and others blocked surveyors' vehicles and deflated their tires as harassment tactics. When the Tuscaroras refused to accept the state's offer to purchase the land, 100 armed state troopers and police invaded Tuscarora lands. The troops were met by a nonviolent front of 150 men, women, and children blocking the road by lying down or standing in front of government trucks. Seneca and Mohawk Indian people set up camps on the disputed land, challenging the state to remove them. Anderson and other leaders were arrested, but the media attention forced the power company to back down. The Federal Power Commission ruled that the Indians did not have to sell the land.

Following the success of the Six Nations people, the Miccosukee Indian Nation of Florida summoned Anderson

In the 1950s, a large number of Iroquois protested the state of New York's hydroelectric projects, which were designed to generate electric power. Pictured here are three Tuscaroras in 1958 protesting a proposed plan to build a 1,383-acre dam that would flood more than one-fifth of their reservation.

to help fight the federal government's attempt to take land from them as part of the Everglades Reclamation Project. In 1959, several hundred Indian people marched on the Bureau of Indian Affairs' headquarters in Washington, D.C., protesting the government policy of the termination of Indian tribes and attempting a citizen's arrest of the BIA commissioner.

All of these protests were predicted by Walter Wetzel, the leader of the Blackfeet Nation of Montana and former president of the National Congress of American Indians: "We

Indians have been struggling unsuccessfully with the problems of maintaining home and family and Indian ownership of the land. We must strike."[8] In addition, "Mad Bear" Anderson, who turned back the bulldozers when a dam was planned on Iroquois land, foretold the new Indian activism. Anderson stated, "Our people were murdered in this country. And they are still being murdered. . . . There is an Indian nationalist movement in the country. I am one of the founders. We are not going to pull any punches from here on in."[9]

A TIME FOR CHANGE

The 1960s were heady years in the United States, as various racial and minority groups struggled to ensure that they received the civil rights to which they were entitled. Leaders such as Dr. Martin Luther King Jr. focused the nation's attention on the discrimination against African Americans. Feminist groups under the leadership of women such as Betty Friedan worked for the congressional passage of the Equal Rights Amendment. American Indian people, under the leadership of men including Richard Oakes, formed such groups as Indians of All Tribes and the American Indian Movement to aggressively pursue their own rights. For the first time in this nation's history, leadership in minority communities came from within the ranks of the oppressed rather than from outside organizations.

The Red Power movement was part of the much larger movement for social change that began within the framework of the social movements of the 1950s. The movement was largely a manifestation of the unrest among blacks, Hispanics, and women who rejected the lifestyles of their parents. College students from the baby-boom generation turned to radical political activity and forms of sexual behavior, music, and dress that shocked their parents.

The lessons of the civil rights movement were not ignored by Indian people. As civil rights issues and rhetoric dominated the headlines, Indian groups adopted the vocabulary and techniques of the Black Power movement in order to ensure that the media presented the issues and concerns of the American Indian to the American public. The National Indian Youth Council (NIYC), a group of young college-educated Indians who organized following the 1961 American Indian Charter Convention in Chicago, adopted some of the ideas of the civil rights movement. They held numerous "fish-ins" along the rivers of the Pacific Northwest, particularly along the Nisqually and Puyallup, where the state of Washington was attempting to use state laws to restrict guaranteed Indian fishing rights. The fish-in demonstrations provided Indian youth in Washington State an opportunity to express their disillusionment and dissatisfaction with U.S. society and also to actively protest the social conditions endured by their people.

Of equal concern to Indian people was the Vietnam War, in which Indian men and women fought to defend a concept of freedom that they themselves had never experienced. American Indians returning from Vietnam were faced with difficult choices. Those who attempted to return to life on the reservation had to deal with high unemployment, poor health facilities, and substandard housing conditions. Those who elected to relocate to urban areas encountered "double discrimination." First, they were faced with the continuing discrimination against Indian people that resulted in high unemployment, police brutality, alcoholism, and often untimely death. Secondly, the returning veterans experienced the discrimination being felt by other Vietnam veterans who were viewed as willing participants in an unpopular war. In an attempt to acquire skills for future employment, many of these Indian veterans used their GI Bill loans and enrolled in colleges in the San Francisco Bay Area. Indian students from these colleges, many of them Vietnam veterans, filled the ranks of the rising Indian activism movement that by this time was called Red Power.

For many Native Americans, life on the reservation was often difficult: High unemployment, poor health facilities, and substandard housing were just some of the problems they had to deal with. Pictured here is a log house on South Dakota's Pine Ridge Reservation, which is indicative of the conditions they had to endure.

The Red Power movement was organized by disillusioned Indian youth from reservations, urban centers, and universities who sought to improve their lives and to reform the conditions of their people. They were speaking out against the treatment Indians were receiving from the local, state, and federal governments, both in the cities and on the reservations. Native American scholar Vine Deloria Jr. stated, "The power movements which had sprung up after 1966 now began to affect Indians, and the center of action was the urban areas on the West Coast, where there was a large

Indian population."[10] The NIYC emphasized the psychological impact of powerlessness on Indian youth in connection with the need for self-determination.

The rhetoric of Indian self-determination can also be traced to the early 1960s, when Melvin Thom, cofounder and president of the NIYC, recognized the need to alleviate the poverty, unemployment, and degrading lifestyles forced on both urban and reservation Indians. Thom said, "We know the odds are against us, but we also realize that we are fighting for the lives of future Indian generations. . . . No people in this world ever have been exterminated without putting up a last resistance. The Indians are gathering."[11]

THE URBANIZATION OF THE AMERICAN INDIAN

In 1960, more than 50 percent of American Indians lived in cities. This trend toward urbanization of the American Indian population began during World War II as a result of wartime industrial job opportunities, federal Indian urban relocation programs, and the general urbanization of the U.S. population as a whole. Many Native Americans migrated to the San Francisco Bay Area during this time to work in defense industries. Because of the industrial need fed by the war, and in keeping with federal policies of relocation, the termination of tribal rights, and the assimilation of Indians into non-Indian society, the federal government also relocated thousands of Indian workers to San Francisco. In the Bay Area, which was one of the largest of more than a dozen relocation sites, the newly urban Indians formed their own organizations to provide the support that the government had promised but failed to give. While some groups were known by tribal names such as the Sioux Club and the Navajo Club, there were also a variety of intertribal organizations, such as sports clubs, dance clubs, and the very early urban powwow clubs. Eventually, some 30 Bay Area social clubs were formed to meet the needs of the urban Indians and their children—children who would, in the 1960s, want the opportunity to go to college and better themselves.

Many urban Indians who were involved with these organizations were dissatisfied with economic and social conditions within both the cities and reservations. They were also disturbed by the lack of self-determination in both communities and by federal policies governing Indian affairs. They represented a population that was poised on the brink of activism: disillusioned Indian youth from reservations, urban centers, and universities who called for reform. In 1968, the United Native Americans (UNA) established *Warpath*, the first militant, pan-Indian newspaper in the United States. A column in the newspaper summed up the attitude of the Bay Area Indian community:

> The "Stoic, Silent Redman" of the past who turned the other cheek to white injustice is dead. (He died of frustration and heartbreak.) And in his place is an angry group of Indians who dare to speak up and voice their dissatisfaction at the world around them. Hate and despair have taken their toll and only action can quiet this smoldering anger that has fused this new Indian movement into being.[12]

SELF-DETERMINATION

It was within the framework of this growing civil rights movement that, in March 1966, President Lyndon Johnson proposed a "new goal for our Indian programs; a goal that ends the old debate about termination of Indian programs and stresses self-determination; a goal that erases old attitudes of paternalism and promotes partnership and self-help."[13] Then, on April 11, 1969, to address the concerns of city-dwelling Indians further, the National Council on Indian Opportunity (NCIO) conducted a public forum before the Committee on Urban Indians in San Francisco. The purpose of the forum was to gain as much information as possible on the condition of American Indians living in the Bay Area, thereby helping to find solutions to their problems and ease tensions that were rising among young urban Indians.

The hearings began with a scathing rebuke by the Reverend Tony Calaman, founder of Freedom for Adoptive Children. Reverend Calaman attacked the San Francisco Police Department, the California Department of Social Welfare, and the Indian child placement system, stating that the non-Indian system emasculated Indian people. When asked to explain, Reverend Calaman described the actions of the Social Welfare Department and the San Francisco Police Department: "The social workers are doing it [emasculation] and the police officers are doing it when they club you on the head. It is a racist institution, just pure racism—and you all know what racism is, and you all know what racists are. Look in the mirror, and you will see a racist."[14]

Earl Livermore, director of the San Francisco American Indian Center, was next to appear before the committee. His testimony was focused on problems Indian people faced in adjusting to urban living, particularly Indian students who had to deal with unfavorable conditions in the public school system. Those conditions ranged from the lack of understanding by school officials to false and misleading statements in school textbooks. Livermore pointed out that many textbooks damaged the Indian child's sense of identity and personal worth. His testimony also touched on urban Indian health problems, which often were the result of the population not having been properly oriented to urban living, and the resulting frustration and depression. Lack of education, according to Livermore, resulted in unemployment. Unemployment led to depression. And depression led Indian people deeper into the depths of despair. Alcoholism, poor nutrition, and inadequate housing were also highlighted as major problems.

A total of 37 Indian people took advantage of the opportunity to appear at the public forum to address the problems and frustrations felt by urban Indian people. LaDonna Harris, a Comanche Indian and chairperson of the Committee on Indian Affairs, summarized the feelings of those in attendance: "[The] non-Indian public does not know this [the problems faced by urban Indians], and it is not an Indian problem. . . . We have been studied to death, and we have been looked at, but still nobody knows. The message does not get across." When asked whether the Red Power movement would become militant, Harris replied, "Heavens, I hope we will."[15]

As mentioned previously, the activism predicted by Harris actually began to build in the 1950s, with more than 20 major events involving demonstrations or nonviolent protests by Indian people. The demonstrations were aimed at ending further reductions of the Indian land base, stopping the termination of Indian tribes, and halting brutality and insensitivity toward Indian people. The militancy at that time, however, was primarily a phenomenon of "traditional" people, typified by the participation of elders, medicine people, and entire communities. It was not the forging of alliances outside of tribal boundaries, such as would later occur during the occupation of San Francisco's Alcatraz Island from 1969 to 1971.

In addition to those individuals who spoke out during the public forum, other Bay Area Indian community members were also raising concerns. Richard McKenzie, a Sioux Indian who was one of the members of a short-lived 1964 Alcatraz occupation party, recognized the uniqueness of the Indian situation and the need to separate it from the black civil rights movement of the period. In a 1969 meeting at the San Francisco Indian Center, McKenzie said, "Kneel-Ins, Sit-Ins, Sleep-Ins, Eat-Ins, Pray-Ins like the Negroes do, wouldn't help us. We would have to occupy the government buildings before things would change."[16]

ALCATRAZ

It was within the context of this more active younger generation of protestors that the first "invasion" of Alcatraz Island took place in 1964. That year, a Lakota woman named Belvia Cottier recalled having read the Fort Laramie Treaty of 1868, which stated that unused federal lands could be reclaimed by Indian people. Cottier and a cousin went to the San Francisco Public Library and obtained a copy of that treaty. Using their own interpretation, they encouraged six Sioux men— Garfield Spotted Elk, Walter Means, Richard McKenzie, Mark Martinez, and Allen Cottier—to reclaim Alcatraz Island in the name of the Lakota people. On March 9, 1964, the men took a boat to Alcatraz, drove claims sticks into the rocky surface, reclaimed the island for four hours, and declared that a cultural center and university should be established on the island. The prison on Alcatraz closed in 1963 and the island was populated only by a caretaker and various species of birds.

One of the Sioux men, Richard McKenzie, pursued the claim for title to the island through the federal court system, but ultimately the case was dismissed due to lack of prosecution on the part of McKenzie. It became obvious to McKenzie's lawyers that the Indians could not win the case because the original treaty stated that Lakota people who were descendents of the 1868 Fort Laramie Treaty could only reclaim unused federal land adjacent to the Great Sioux Reservation in South Dakota. It would be impossible to stretch any interpretation to include land in the state of California.

Then, on November 20, 1969, following the unsuccessful occupation attempt in 1964 and one that had occurred earlier that November, a group of Native American students from various California universities, with support from Bay Area Indian organizations and leaders, began the 19-month occupation of Alcatraz Island. Today, the Indian people whose lives were most affected by the occupation regard it as perhaps the most important event in the postreservation struggle for Indian land, treaty, and civil rights. Nearly 30 years after the occupation, many historians identify the 1969 occupation of Alcatraz Island as the spark that ignited the Red Power movement of the 1970s.

THE RISE OF PROTEST GROUPS

New Indian organizations also began to form during this period to support the growing activism and provide a voice for the rising militancy. In 1964, the Survival of American Indians Association (SAIA) grew out of the Pacific Northwest fish-ins. Then, on July 28, 1968, the American Indian Movement (AIM) was founded in Minneapolis, Minnesota. AIM initially concentrated on eliminating the discriminatory practices of local city government in the areas of employment and housing, but more specifically on halting police brutality toward urban Indian people. In the summer of 1968, United Native Americans (UNA) was founded in the San Francisco Bay Area. UNA had a pan-Indian focus and sought to unify all persons of Indian blood throughout the Americas. Its goal was to promote self-determination through Indian control of Indian affairs at every level.

The year 1968 closed with a confrontation between Canada, the United States, and members of the Iroquois Nation. Canada had restricted the free movement of Mohawk Indians between the United States and Canada, demanding that Mohawks pay tolls to use the Cornwall International Bridge and pay customs taxes on goods brought back from the United States. Members of the Iroquois League felt that this was an infringement of their treaty rights granted by Great Britain, and members of the Mohawk tribe confronted Canadian

Although the terms of the 1794 Jay Treaty had guaranteed the Iroquois the right to travel freely across the U.S. border with Canada, they have not always been able to do so. In the 1960s, the Canadian government attempted to make them pay tolls to use the Cornwall International Bridge, which connects Cornwall, Ontario, with Massena, New York. Pictured here are members of the Indian Defense League of America marching across the bridge shortly after Canada recognized their right to cross the bridge freely in 1969.

officials as a means of forcing the issues of tolls and customs collections on the bridge. The protest specifically dealt with Canada's failure to honor the Jay Treaty of 1794 between itself and the United States (which permitted the Mohawks to transport goods between the two nations).

In addition to the rise in activism among the Mohawks, the Miccosukees, the Bay Area Indians, and the Taos Pueblo

Indians of New Mexico also reasserted their claims to ancestral lands. On August 13, 1951, Taos Indians had filed a suit before the Indian Claims Commission, seeking support for the validity of title to Taos Blue Lake. On September 8, 1965, the Indian Claims Commission affirmed that the U.S. government took the area unjustly from its rightful owners, the Taos Pueblo. During the ceremony that returned Blue Lake to the Taos people, President Richard Nixon spoke of the contribution of American Indian people who had given such great character to the United States. The return of Taos Blue Lake would become the centerpiece of Indian policy for Nixon's administration.

President Nixon saw the return of Blue Lake as an opportunity to put into action his support for Indian self-determination. Nixon had many opponents in Congress who had little if any concern for the rights of Indian people and who were more concerned about the support of the non-Indian electorate. Nixon's detractors felt that returning land to the Taos people would set a bad precedent and result in a backlash in the polls.

President Nixon and members of his White House staff had to badger and plead for support for the bill that would return the sacred Blue Lake. This 1970 bill came at the same time that Congress was set to approve a new intercontinental ballistic missile reduction treaty with the Soviet Union. Nixon added his support to those who wanted to see the treaty passed in return for their support for the return of Blue Lake. Both the treaty and the Blue Lake bill became law.

NIXON'S PLAN

On September 27, 1968, then-presidential candidate Richard Nixon sent a message to the delegates of the National Congress of American Indians (NCAI), who were attending their annual convention in Omaha, Nebraska. He stated, "The sad plight of the American Indian is a stain on the honor of the American

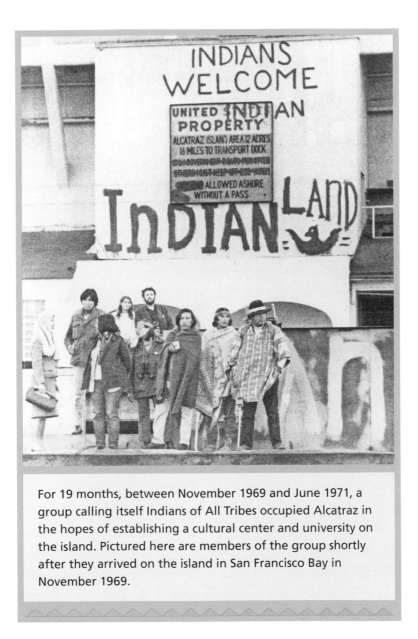

For 19 months, between November 1969 and June 1971, a group calling itself Indians of All Tribes occupied Alcatraz in the hopes of establishing a cultural center and university on the island. Pictured here are members of the group shortly after they arrived on the island in San Francisco Bay in November 1969.

people."[17] Nixon proposed a bold new plan for Indian self-determination that would officially bring the termination era to an end and transfer responsibility for tribal affairs from the federal government to Indian people. Nixon promised that, if he were elected, "the right of self-determination of the Indian people will be respected and their participation in planning their own destiny will be encouraged."[18]

Nixon's policy of self-determination would also be tested in California, particularly in the Bay Area. In 1969, the Native American Student Union (NASU) formed in California, bringing together a new pan-Indian alliance among newly emerging Native American studies programs on various college campuses. In San Francisco, NASU members prepared to test Nixon's commitment to self-determination before a national audience by once again occupying Alcatraz Island with the battle cry "We Hold The Rock!" Richard Oakes would be identified as the leader of the occupation, LaNada Boyer would be the only person to participate for the entire 19 months, and Dennis Turner, another member of the union, would become a member of the Indian council on the island. For Indian people of the Bay Area, the social movements of the 1960s had come to full maturity. The heightened social awareness generated by the Black Power movement, the new left generation, the third-world strikes, and the emerging La Raza movement provided a sympathetic national audience for a new Indian activism. In November 1969, Indian people moved onto the national scene of ethnic unrest as active participants in a war of their own. Alcatraz Island was the battlefield, and although the occupation came to an end before all the goals were met, it served as a powerful symbol of Indian self-determination and was a springboard for other future battles, including the occupation at Wounded Knee several years later.

4

Murder on the "Res"

IN FEBRUARY 1972, RAYMOND YELLOW THUNDER, A 51-year-old Lakota from the Pine Ridge Reservation, was abducted by two white men in Gordon, Nebraska, for no apparent reason other than he was an Indian. After forcing Yellow Thunder to drink alcohol, they stripped him naked from the waist down and threw him in an American Legion hall where a dance was in progress. He was forced to dance for those in attendance and was then thrown out of the hall and beaten. Eight days later, two young boys found his battered and lifeless body in the cab of a pickup truck in a used-car lot in Gordon. An autopsy attributed his death to a cerebral hemorrhage. He had been dead for more than two days. In a preliminary report, Sheridan County attorney Michael V. Smith called the incident at the American Legion hall "a very cruel practical joke." Nearly two weeks after Yellow Thunder was shoved onto the dance-hall floor, four men and one woman, all white, were arrested and charged in the incident. Two were charged with false imprisonment; two with false imprisonment and manslaughter; and the fifth with manslaughter.

DATELINE: GORDON, NEBRASKA

Attacks on Indian people by white racists were not uncommon on the Pine Ridge Reservation or in Gordon. With a population of some 1,200 residents, Gordon was a small rural town reminiscent of countless others throughout the Great Plains states. These towns were known locally as "a white man's town," and the fact that Gordon was a "white town," sharing a boundary with an Indian reservation dominated the way of life. Roughly 10 percent of Gordon's population was Indian, but that fluctuated as people came and went across the border to the Pine Ridge Reservation. Indians went to Gordon to look for work and to shop. The near total absence of places to shop on the reservation and the prohibition of the sale of alcohol there brought a steady flow of Indians to Gordon and other nearby towns. There were charges by Indians of police brutality in Gordon, and accusations that Indians were arrested far in excess of their

THE MOCCASIN TELEGRAPH

The "moccasin telegraph" is an unofficial system of communication that originated on Indian reservations and later became a primary means of communication among Indian people in urban areas. The moccasin telegraph works in much the same way as a modern "phone tree" notification system, whereby one person tells two or three individuals of an event or rumor, and those two or three notify two or three other individuals, so that within only a few hours literally hundreds of people will have heard the original transmission. It was through the use of the moccasin telegraph that Indian people were kept informed of the movements of tribal chairman Dicky Wilson and his GOON squad.

percentage of the overall population. The police largely ignored the situation and the mostly white roster of judges in the area refused to try whites for crimes against Indians. Jail cells in Gordon were disproportionately filled with Indian people who had run afoul of racist law enforcement officers.

Information on the "moccasin telegraph" traveled fast on Indian reservations, and rumors about the condition of Raymond Yellow Thunder's body spread throughout Indian country. It was rumored that Yellow Thunder's body bore evidence of mutilation and that his skull had been fractured by a blow from a blunt instrument. There were demands that his body be exhumed and that a second autopsy be performed. Smith, the county attorney, denied all rumors. Local Indian people were incensed with this perceived miscarriage of justice. An Indian man who may have been involved in a much less violent crime would have been charged with murder, they claimed. Local arrest records verify that this was the case. Indian people were almost always charged with the most serious indictment for a particular crime and always served time in jail, frequently in the Nebraska State Penitentiary, where the ratio of Indian prisoners (per population) far exceeded the ratio of non-Indian prisoners. Negative images of Indians as either worthless alcoholics or crazed warriors about to go on the warpath could be found daily in Nebraska newspapers and magazines. Indians were portrayed as lazy and unreliable. Those same publications failed to note that unemployment rates of Native Americans exceeded 40 percent on reservations, while those who found work were paid substandard income. They also failed to note the high infant mortality rate and the low life-expectancy rate.

DICKY WILSON AND PINE RIDGE

As a result of this media treatment and the failure of the U.S. government to live up to legal treaty obligations, Native American elders asked members of the American Indian

In 1972, pro-BIA chairman Richard "Dicky" Wilson was elected head of the Oglala Sioux Nation. Wilson (left) is pictured here with Chief U.S. Marshal Wayne Colburn on March 27, 1973, during the Wounded Knee occupation.

Movement (AIM) to come to the reservation to protest Nebraska's treatment of Indians and counter the violence being inflicted on the traditional people by the pro-BIA chairman of the Oglala Sioux Nation, Richard "Dicky" Wilson and his GOON (Guardians Of the Oglala Nation) squad. The invitation extended to AIM to intervene on the Pine Ridge Reservation is indicative of the gravity of the situation. By and large, traditional Indian elders had little respect for AIM. The time-honored approach to problem solving was through negotiation and consensus, while traditional leaders recognized AIM as a militant, armed warrior society. The U.S. government categorized AIM as an armed subversive group that sought to overthrow the federal government. Drive-by shootings, beatings, and murders of traditional people, as well as of AIM members who opposed Dicky Wilson and his GOON squad–run tribal government, were common occurrences.

At the time, the Pine Ridge Reservation had the highest murder rate in the United States. The ratio of FBI agents to citizens was also higher than anywhere else in the country. Reservation residents claimed that more than 200 Indian people had been murdered or disappeared without a trace from the reservation after Wilson became tribal chairman in 1972. The FBI agents did not investigate those deaths; rather, they were used to further support Wilson and the GOON squad against the traditional Indian people. The period became known as "the reign of terror." Indian people feared for their lives, knowing that Wilson, the GOON squad, and the FBI were in a lethal partnership against them. The FBI claimed that it could not be held accountable for any deaths that occurred while agents were doing their job.

SEEKING JUSTICE

Members of AIM arrived in Gordon on March 1, 1972. AIM leader Russell Means, himself an Oglala Sioux, announced: "We intend to put it [the treatment of Indian people in Gordon] in the national spotlight and expose the racist state of Nebraska."[19] After the announcement, AIM members staged a march of solidarity down Gordon's Main Street. The Indians, including Means and fellow AIM leader Dennis Banks, went to the Gordon town hall to hear testimony of police brutality and harassment. On March 7, a 12-member, all-Indian grand jury was chosen from among the 1,000 Indians who had by that time converged on Gordon from across Nebraska and South Dakota. The allegations heard by the grand jury were presented to city officials, who agreed to establish a biracial human relations council.

On January 21, 1973, manslaughter charges were filed in Buffalo Gap, South Dakota, against Harold Schmidt, a white man who had murdered Wesley Bad Heart Bull, a 20-year-old Oglala Sioux. AIM members protested the lighter-than-expected sentence after the charges against Schmidt were reduced to involuntary manslaughter, and he served only one day in jail. After being pushed down the courthouse steps in Custer, South Dakota, Wesley's mother, Sarah, served five months of a one- to five-year sentence for protesting Schmidt's sentence. Because of the violent treatment dealt to Sarah Bad Heart Bull, a confrontational protest occurred and the courthouse and chamber of commerce buildings in Custer were set on fire. The FBI at this time identified AIM as an armed subversive militant group and increased the numbers of surveillance teams that were assigned to monitor all AIM activities and the movements of its leadership. AIM and its leadership were placed under surveillance under the U.S. government's Counter Intelligence Program (COUNTERINTELPRO). Undercover FBI agents were sent to infiltrate AIM and to gather evidence for prosecution.

The U.S. government perfected the use of the Counter Intelligence Program in the 1950s and 1960s while pursuing the Black Panther Party and its leaders. A common practice of COUNTERINTELPRO was to plant one or more informants in the heart of the target organization. Informants were members of the same racial group as those of the organization that the government sought to infiltrate. To find informants, FBI agents would locate people who had police records and were awaiting trial for additional offenses. Federal prosecutors would agree to waive the charges and any jail or prison time in exchange for infiltrating the group and providing information.

The federal government planted three COUNTERINTELPRO agents in the American Indian Movement. One of those was Douglas Durham, a Lakota who earned great trust and rose to the position of personal bodyguard and driver for AIM leader Russell Means. Durham was able to provide moment-to-moment information to the FBI about AIM's plans.

Another tactic of COUNTERINTELPRO was a skill they called "bad-jacketing." This was a method in which they planted false rumors about individuals within an organization and created distrust, disharmony, and ultimately chaos. One victim of bad-jacketing was Anna Mae Aquash. She was a loyal AIM member and activist, but a rumor was planted that she was an FBI informant. In 1976, Aquash was killed alongside a road on the Pine Ridge Reservation (see page 56).

MURDERS AT PINE RIDGE

On February 27, 1973, AIM leaders and about 200 Indian supporters were en route to Porcupine, South Dakota. Wilson and his GOON squad were armed and waiting for their entrance into town. Rather than entering Porcupine, though, one of the women suggested that the caravan drive directly to the village of Wounded Knee, the sight of the 1890 massacre of 300 Lakota men, women, and children. Wilson and his squad were left armed and waiting while the caravan of 54 cars carrying about 250 AIM members and supporters occupied the Wounded Knee trading post, museum, gas station, and two churches. The occupation marked the beginning of an armed conflict between AIM and the U.S. government that lasted until May 8, 1973.

But the occupation did not bring an end to the murders on Pine Ridge Reservation. The names of the 57 Indian people whom the FBI acknowledges were killed on Pine Ridge sound like a list of those who were killed at Wounded Knee Creek in December 1890: Swift Bird, Cut Grass, Slow Beat, Standing Soldier, Eagle Hawk (and her two children), White Plume, Sam Afraid of Bear, Spotted Elk, Black Elk. Perhaps the most significant and controversial murder occurred in 1975, the trials for which were still taking place in 2007. The victim's name was Anna Mae Pictou Aquash. Indian people believe that the FBI set up Aquash for murder by planting information that she was an informant against AIM. The FBI, in keeping with the investigations of the more than 200 murders on the

Pine Ridge Reservation, said that the government had "clean hands" and that it was in no way involved in using her as an informant.

Anna Mae Pictou Aquash

Anna Mae Pictou Aquash was a Micmac Indian who was born in Nova Scotia, Canada, on March 27, 1945. She was an activist who joined AIM in the early 1970s and worked with the organization until she was murdered (some say executed) on the Pine Ridge Reservation in 1976. At the age of 17, Aquash and her common-law husband, Jake Maloney, a fellow Micmac, left the poverty of the reservation and moved to Boston in 1962. Aquash soon gave birth to two daughters, Denise and Deborah. The birth of the girls prompted Maloney and Aquash to move to a Micmac reservation in the Province of Nova Scotia so that the children could become acquainted with their Indian heritage.

Aquash and Maloney eventually broke off their marriage, and in 1968, Aquash moved back to Boston, where she worked in a factory and volunteered at the Boston Indian Council's headquarters. It was there that she was exposed to the ravages of alcoholism through her work with young urban Indians, who often turned to alcohol to ease depression, and first heard of the American Indian Movement. By 1970, AIM had moved to the forefront as the primary activist group for Native Americans. As noted in Chapter 3, an earlier group, Indians of All Tribes, had occupied Alcatraz Island from 1969 to 1971 and had informed the nation of the broken treaties, the loss of Indian land, and the cultural genocide being carried out against Indian people.

On November 26, 1970, Russell Means led AIM in seizing control of the *Mayflower II* in Plymouth, Massachusetts. Means and members of 25 Indian tribes proclaimed Thanksgiving a national day of mourning to protest the taking of Native American lands by white colonists. The occupiers gave

In early November 1972, participants in the Trail of Broken
Treaties, which was a cross-country protest to bring about
awareness of such Native American issues as treaty rights,
living standards, and inadequate housing, reached their
destination—Washington, D.C. Upon arriving in the nation's
capital, they occupied the headquarters of the Bureau
of Indian Affairs (BIA) for 71 hours before finally being
dispersed on November 9.

credit to the occupation of Alcatraz Island as the symbol of a
newly awakened desire of the Indians for unity and authority
in the white world.

Aquash participated in the protest and the event made
her even more determined to work for Native American
rights. She had found a cause on which she could focus her
energies. Along with her new husband, Nogeeshik, whom
she met in Boston, Aquash participated in the 1972 Trail
of Broken Treaties, a protest march on Washington, D.C.
The march was in fact a caravan that originated on Alcatraz
Island following the death of Richard Oakes, spokesperson
for the Alcatraz occupation, and resulted in the 71-hour

occupation of the Bureau of Indian Affairs' (BIA) headquarters. AIM leaders presented a 20-point Indian Manifesto demanding redress of wrongs against Indian nations and people.

Aquash, by this time a full member of AIM, traveled to the Pine Ridge Reservation and joined with AIM in the 1973 occupation of Wounded Knee. Following that occupation, Aquash's credibility and participation in AIM increased. In

TRAIL OF BROKEN TREATIES: 20-POINT INDIAN MANIFESTO

1. Restoration of treaty making (ended by Congress in 1871)

2. Establishment of a treaty commission to make new treaties (with Indian nations)

3. Indian leaders to address Congress

4. Review of treaty commitments and violations

5. Non-ratified treaties to go before the Senate (primarily California Indian treaties)

6. All Indians to be governed by treaty relations

7. Relief for Native American nations for treaty rights violations

8. Recognition of the right of Indians to interpret treaties

9. Joint congressional committee to be formed on reconstruction of Indian relations

10. Restoration of 110 million acres of land taken from Native American nations by the United States

1975, she and fellow AIM member Leonard Peltier traveled to Farmington, New Mexico, to an AIM conference held in support of Dine (Navajo) Indians who were protesting against coal mining on their traditional lands. It appears that it was while in Farmington that Aquash was first accused of being an FBI operative within the AIM organization. AIM members Dino Butler and Robert Robideau confronted her at that

11. Restoration of terminated rights (tribes that had undergone the Termination Act)

12. Repeal of state jurisdiction (Public Law 280) on Native American nations

13. Federal protection for offenses against Indians

14. Abolishment of the Bureau of Indian Affairs

15. Creation of a new office of Federal Indian Relations

16. New office to remedy breakdown in the constitutionally prescribed relationship between the United States and Indian nations

17. Indian nations to be immune to commerce regulation, taxes, and trade restrictions of states

18. Protection of Indian religious freedom and cultural integrity

19. Establishment of national Indian voting with local options; free national Indian organizations from governmental controls

20. Reclaim and affirm health, housing, employment, economic development, and education for all Indian people

convention and, according to Robideau, "the three of us walked away satisfied she was not an agent."[20] This appears to be true because Aquash was called back to Pine Ridge to help organize security for Lakota traditionalists and AIM supporters who were being attacked by Dicky Wilson and his GOON squad. On June 26, 1975, while Aquash and other AIM members were camped on the Jumping Bull family land on the Pine Ridge Reservation, a firefight broke out between AIM members and FBI agents who were allegedly attempting to serve a warrant on an AIM member thought to be guilty of stealing a pair of cowboy boots. During the firefight, two FBI agents, Ronald Williams and Jack Coler, and a young Indian man, Joe Stuntz, were killed. AIM members, fully aware that they would be the subject of a no-holds-barred, relentless search for the shooters of Williams and Coler, dispersed across the United States and into Canada and went into hiding.

On February 24, 1976, Aquash's body was found by a rancher alongside State Road 73 on the far northeastern corner of the Pine Ridge Reservation. The condition of the body indicated that she had been dead for some time, probably about 10 days. This was later confirmed. Aquash's body was initially taken to the Pine Ridge Public Health Service, where BIA medical practitioner W. O. Brown performed an autopsy. Brown stated that the cause of death was exposure. During the autopsy, federal agents who knew Aquash were present, but she was not identified and her body was buried. However, her hands were first cut off and sent to the FBI for a fingerprint analysis, and a week later, "Jane Doe" was identified as Anna Mae Aquash. Her family did not believe that she died from exposure and on March 10, 1976, her body was exhumed. Dr. Garry Peterson, an independent pathologist from Minneapolis, conducted a second autopsy the following day. This autopsy revealed that her death resulted from a bullet that entered the back of the head.

In the years since 1976, much speculation has surrounded Aquash's death. The FBI claims that AIM members executed her when they came to believe that she was an FBI informant, but the FBI denies that she ever worked for or with the government. AIM members have claimed that the FBI executed Aquash just as they had numerous AIM troublemakers on the Pine Ridge Reservation.

In the most recent turn of events, on March 20, 2003, two men were indicted for her murder: Fritz Arlo Looking Cloud, a Lakota, and John Graham, a Southern Tutchone Athabascan from Canada. On February 8, 2004, Arlo Looking Cloud was tried before a U.S. federal jury and was found guilty and given a mandatory sentence of life in prison, even though no physical evidence linking him to the crime was presented. A videotape was introduced into evidence at the trial in which Looking Cloud admitted to being present at the time of the murder but claims that Graham was the shooter. Graham denies any involvement in the shooting death of Aquash and claims that when he last saw her she was alive and en route from Denver to the Pine Ridge Indian Reservation. As of early 2007, Graham was free on bail and awaiting an appeal of an extradition hearing that would return him to the United States to stand trial.

Aquash's murder, while tragic, is different from other murders on the Pine Ridge Reservation in one respect: Her death was investigated. Depending on the source of one's information, the number of uninvestigated deaths runs anywhere from 75 to as many as 225. The latter number is based on the number of Indian people who were killed or simply vanished in the years between 1965 and 1975.

Mysterious Deaths of AIM Members

One such mysterious death was that of was Priscilla White Plume, an AIM supporter who was killed on September 28, 1973. The cause of death as determined by the coroner was blunt force trauma to the skull. AIM members claimed that White Plume was killed in Anderson, South Dakota, by members of Dicky Wilson's GOON squad because of her criticism of Wilson and her active support of AIM. The FBI issued a statement that they believed White Plume had been struck and killed by a vehicle in a hit-and-run accident. The FBI not only declined to prosecute the case, because there was insufficient evidence to establish a federal crime, but also declined to investigate White Plume's death any further. No vehicle was ever produced that would have supported the FBI's version of the death.

The death of Clarence Cross is even more disturbing. On July 11, 1973, Cross's car was stopped by GOON squad members and he was shot to death when he and his brother Vernal refused to leave their car. Vernal Cross was wounded, survived, and was able to identify the assailants. Clarence Cross was shot in the stomach and right thigh and ultimately died of complications of those injuries at Fitzsimons Army Medical Center in Aurora, Colorado. The U.S. Attorney's Office advised that there was insufficient evidence that a crime had been committed and the officers involved in the shooting were never charged with a crime.

The death of Andrew Paul Stewart is equally troubling. Stewart was the nephew of AIM spiritual leader Leonard Crow Dog. Members of Dicky Wilson's GOON squad targeted Crow Dog for not only providing spiritual leadership for AIM members, but also because he was suspected of harboring AIM members being sought by the FBI. On July 26, 1975, a BIA officer on the Rosebud Indian Reservation in South Dakota announced that Stewart had been declared dead on arrival at the Rosebud Public Health Service Hospital. Preliminary findings for cause of death were that he had died from a gunshot wound to the head. The results of the official autopsy stated that the cause of death "was probably a self-inflicted gunshot wound." Based on this report, no follow-up investigation was conducted even though AIM members charged that Stewart had been shot by either the FBI or GOON squad members. The FBI stated that "no credible information" was developed suggesting that any specific person caused the death. The case was subsequently closed.

The deaths of Robert Reddy and Melvin Spider are examples of murders in which suspects were identified but the FBI chose not to charge them with the deaths. Reddy was found dead on December 16, 1975, on the Pine Ridge Indian Reservation. The official autopsy revealed that Reddy died from two stab wounds through his heart. The FBI, though it was provided with a suspect, determined that insufficient evidence was available to prosecute. No further investigation was undertaken.

Spider, an AIM member, was found dead on the Pine Ridge Reservation by a member of Wilson's GOON squad. The officer notified the FBI and requested assistance with the investigation. The initial investigation indicated that Spider had most likely died as the result of trauma from a hit-and-run accident. An autopsy was conducted on September 23, 1973, which indicated the cause of death to be "external cerebral lacerations of the brain, which were traumatic in nature, the cause of which was not obvious."[21] AIM members claimed that Spider had been run down and killed intentionally because of his membership in the group. FBI records indicate that, although a suspect was found, there was insufficient evidence to charge that person with the death. No further investigation was carried out.

The Occupation of "The Knee"

DURING THE SPRING OF 1972, THE BIA BACKED THE questionable election of Richard "Dicky" Wilson as tribal chairman of the Oglala Sioux Nation. Wilson saw his election as validation of his pro-reform Indian government. He split the nation along the lines of progressives and the traditionalists who preferred the old form of Indian tribal leadership. Wilson practiced nepotism (the hiring of relatives and friends) in his doling out of jobs and tribal funds. Traditionalists had no voice in tribal government and were left jobless and destitute. They turned to AIM for support. As noted in the previous chapter, Wilson used tribal funds to hire thugs and form a vigilante police force called the GOON squad (Guardians of the Oglala Nation) who began a reign of terror against AIM and its supporters. Hundreds of people were threatened, beaten, or killed. The homes of Oglala traditionalists and AIM supporters were the targets of drive-by shootings with military assault rifles and in some cases were burned to the ground.

THE GOALS OF THE OCCUPATION

Wilson offered a threat and a challenge to AIM leader Dennis Banks, stating that he would cut off Banks's hair braids if Banks set foot on the Pine Ridge Reservation. By February 1973, a major confrontation was brewing.

The goals of the occupation as outlined by AIM leaders included support for the reformation of tribal government, as well as bringing attention to Native American grievances. Russell Means requested a congressional investigation into conditions on all Indian reservations, as well as into the corruption Indian people believed was rampant in the BIA. Treaty provisions that included housing assistance, medical care, and schooling for reservation children went unfulfilled. AIM leaders specifically wanted a hearing to take place concerning these treaty violations and the reinstitution of treaty making and treaty rights that had formally ended in 1871.

THE U.S. GOVERNMENT REACTS

The Nixon White House, the Department of Defense, and the Department of Justice coordinated efforts throughout the Wounded Knee occupation. Where the occupation of Alcatraz Island had been nonviolent, the Wounded Knee occupants were armed and considered dangerous. The U.S. government decided that it could not assume a waiting posture as it had at Alcatraz. Weapons, personnel, and equipment, some of which had been used in Vietnam, were supplied by the Department of Defense. Because the land was Indian country, the federal government held jurisdiction over the reservation, and therefore state and local forces were not authorized to assist in law enforcement. U.S. government security forces and members of the Oglala GOON squad manned roadblocks at entrances to Wounded Knee to prevent access to the area. Their primary objective was to isolate the

During the occupation of Wounded Knee in 1973, Oglala chairman Richard "Dicky" Wilson and his GOON (Guardians of the Oglala Nation) squad set up roadblocks into Pine Ridge Reservation to stop supplies from being delivered to AIM members. Wilson is pictured here with his men at the main entrance to the reservation on March 26, 1973.

occupiers and to stop food, ammunition, and reinforcements from reaching the occupation force, while preventing injuries or deaths if possible.

Gunfire was exchanged between government forces and AIM security throughout the occupation. AIM, relying on the experience of American Indian Vietnam veterans, fortified the area by digging trenches, setting up roadblocks, and establishing day and night foot patrols. During the occupation, U.S. Marshal Lloyd Grimm received a wound that paralyzed him from the waist down. Two Indian men—Frank Clearwater and Lawrence Lamont—were killed during the occupation. Clearwater, a Cherokee, received a fatal wound while asleep on a cot in an occupied church during a period of gunfire exchange. AIM supporters evacuated him from the village but he died in the hospital on April 25. Lamont, a Lakota resident of the Pine Ridge Reservation, received a fatal gunshot wound on April 26. Following the two deaths, both sides agreed upon a tenuous cease-fire. Still, tensions between the occupiers and the federal authorities grew and the situation worsened. Both groups established, violated, and reinstated cease-fires. AIM security, U.S. forces, and, on occasion, the GOON squad were each guilty of instigating gunfire exchanges.

On March 26, some 340 FBI agents and federal marshals surrounded Wounded Knee village. The government forces were by this time covertly supported by weaponry provided by the U.S. Army. Among the munitions and other supplies provided were 17 armored personnel carries, 130,000 rounds of M-16 ammunition, 4,000 rounds of M-1 ammunition, 24,000 flares, 12 M-79 grenade launchers, 600 cases of C-S gas, and 100 rounds of M-40 high explosive rounds, as well as helicopters and Phantom jets. This was all equipment similar to that being used simultaneously by U.S. forces in Vietnam.

AIM security marked the first days of the occupation by digging bunkers with connecting trenches, setting up roadblocks, and establishing security patrols. They developed and maintained a defensive perimeter around Wounded Knee that included a total of nine bunkers. Trip wires and flares were placed in strategic locations to alert the occupiers to the approach of government troops or members of Wilson's GOON squad.

NEGOTIATING AN END TO THE STANDOFF

Negotiations to end the conflict began almost immediately upon the start of the Wounded Knee takeover and continued throughout the 71-day occupation. The U.S. government and the AIM leadership developed a series of proposals that were rejected by one side or the other. In late March, Kent Frizzell replaced Harlington Wood as the senior U.S. government official at Wounded Knee. Frizzell established contact with Dennis Banks and offered to have justice department personnel hear the alleged civil rights violations. Negotiations between Banks and Frizzell continued for one week, at which time an agreement was signed. The terms of the agreement stated that Russell Means would submit himself for arrest, and any occupiers with an outstanding warrant would also be arrested. Additionally,

GOVERNMENT NEGOTIATION

The word *negotiations* has a different meaning to different people. The U.S. government entered into negotiations with the Indian occupiers of Wounded Knee, just as it did with the Indian occupiers of Alcatraz Island. The government did not intend in either instance to give up anything. It was a ploy, or tactic, used by the government to wage a war of attrition. That is to say, the government had time on its hands. It could wait until the occupiers ran out of food supplies, ammunition, or simply tired of the hardships they were enduring. Because the occupiers at Wounded Knee were considered violent, a tight blockade was instituted. This basically assured that there would be little or nothing in the way of supplies or additional Indian occupiers able to get through to lend strength to the occupying force.

During the early part of the occupation of Wounded Knee, Indian activists built bunkers with connecting trenches, set up roadblocks, and established security patrols to monitor the defensive perimeter around the town. Here, AIM members stand behind a bunker during the occupation.

the Wounded Knee occupiers agreed to lay down their weapons. In response, Frizzell agreed that a meeting would take place between AIM leaders and a representative of the Nixon White House to discuss the possibility of a presidential committee investigation into the violation of Indian treaties.

On April 5, Means disavowed the agreement, stating that AIM leaders would never agree to lay down their weapons until the conclusion of a promised White House meeting. The White House, represented by Frizzell, replied that a possibility, not a promise, of a White House meeting had been made, and that the surrender of weapons prior to the meeting was nonnegotiable. Consequently, negotiations continued. During the period between April 28 and May 5, a series of negotiation sessions took place between the primary parties in the matter—Frizzell, Oglala elders, and AIM. On May 5, Leonard Garment, the senior White House consultant to President Nixon, sent a letter that stated White House representatives would meet with the Lakota leadership to discuss the 1868 Sioux Treaty. In addition to disarmament, though, a new stipulation was added: All persons were required to leave Wounded Knee. The U.S. government agreed to pull back from its position as the occupiers abandoned theirs. Government forces would then search the area, collect any remaining weapons, and destroy all bunkers.

However, several issues pressed the AIM occupiers to end the occupation: lack of food and ammunition, no electrical power, and no medical supplies. Ultimately a timetable was agreed upon between AIM and the federal government that detailed when government forces would be allowed to enter Wounded Knee to collect all weapons. Following that, U.S. forces would transport remaining AIM supporters to a government roadblock, where a team of defense committee lawyers would be present to witness the processing procedure.

THE RESULTS OF THE OCCUPATION

When the occupation of Wounded Knee came to an end on May 8, 1973, there were 237 arrests made and 35 weapons were confiscated. Russell Means and Dennis Banks were arraigned on 10 felony counts in a trial that lasted eight months. Out of the 129 people processed, 110 were American Indians. Federal forces destroyed AIM security bunkers along with government bunkers and completed the evacuation of Wounded Knee by the end of the day. AIM activist and Wounded Knee occupier Carter Camp captured the feeling of many of the occupiers:

We were a strong community. We all had work to do and fighting to do. But at the same time, we could live together and do the things that we wanted to do, say the things that we wanted to say, and understand this world the way that Indian people understand it. So, it made us feel good. We just really were able to come together in a unity that you don't hardly find in Indian country. We're different tribes and we don't always get around each other like that. I mean literally thousands of Indian people were coming from around the country. At any one time we might only have 700 or 800 people in Wounded Knee, but people were coming and leaving. Then, of course, a group of AIM people stayed there throughout the thing.[22]

South Dakota senator James Abourezk, under the authority of the U.S. Senate Subcommittee on Indian Affairs, conducted hearings on the events that led to the confrontation and the occupation of Wounded Knee. After hearing evidence by tribal chairman Richard Wilson and AIM leader Russell Means, Abourezk proposed a joint Senate resolution in order to establish an Indian policy review committee. Its purpose included a review of the legal relationship between Native Americans and the U.S. government and to provide support for the development of more effective policies.

The Nixon White House subsequently broke the agreement that had ended the occupation. On May 13, an aide to President Nixon read a statement that "treaty making with the Indians ended in 1871." AIM demands that the U.S. government investigate the FBI never materialized. Tribal chairman Wilson and his GOON squad members were never prosecuted. Instead, a new reign of terror was carried out against AIM members and their supporters. While the FBI claims that all deaths have been investigated, residents of the Pine Ridge Reservation still live in fear of government forces.

The occupation of Wounded Knee differed from the occupation of Alcatraz in several ways, but most importantly, the public looked at Alcatraz in a more favorable light. Alcatraz had garnered international support; money and donations flowed to the island. In addition, President Nixon stated that the Indians, who were not armed, were not hurting anyone so they should be allowed to remain on Alcatraz. On the other hand, Wounded Knee was seen as a violent takeover. In the words of political activist John Trudell, the Indians at Alcatraz used "body politics." At Wounded Knee it was far different. Both AIM and U.S. government forces were armed and both groups proved that they were more than willing to shoot to kill.

Indian Women at Wounded Knee

THE HISTORY OF AMERICAN INDIAN WOMEN IS LARGELY ignored in our textbooks. Except for Pocahontas, whose real name was Matoaka (meaning "frisky girl"), and Sacagawea, the guide for the Lewis and Clark expedition, Indian women have been relegated to obscure references, almost as an afterthought.

THE IMPORT OF INDIAN WOMEN: THE IROQUOIS

Unfortunately, Indian women who were members of most activists groups of the 1950s, 1960s, and 1970s were also largely ignored. The male gender was the "power gender" during that generation, so it should not surprise the reader that this would be the case. The fact that women are omitted from these written histories does not mean, however, that they did not play key roles in making decisions. They did. Sometimes they also took the male's role as leader and sometimes as armed warrior. Historian Dr. Elizabeth Castle explains this simply: "Women were the backbone and men were the jawbone" of the American Indian Movement.[23]

The refusal to recognize Indian women in power is not a new concept. Upon landing in the New World, the settlers from England set out to "tame the wilderness." What they found, however, was the well-established Iroquois League consisting of five tribes: the Mohawk, Oneida, Onondaga, Cayuga, and Seneca. The English leaders were pleased at what they perceived to be the guiding principle of leadership in this group. There was a leadership council with 50 seats, all filled by men. Only 49 of the seats were filled at any one time, the vacant seat rotating each year among the five tribes in honor of the leader of the league, Deganaweda.

Deganaweda was held in high respect by members of the Iroquois League, because he was the one that the Creator spoke to in a vision. Prior to the formation of the league, the five tribes were in a state of constant warfare. The rule of "blood feud" set the boundaries of warfare: If a tribal member was killed or otherwise incapacitated, it was the responsibility of tribal members to seek revenge through the killing of a member of the offending tribe. Throughout the decades, this had resulted in thousands of deaths and tribes that were near extinction. While in a trance, Deganaweda received a vision from the Creator in which he was given instructions on how to end the blood feud: form the five tribes into a league, each with equal representation. Blood feuds were to be ended and everyone was to adopt a dedication to the "tree of peace." Although each tribe belonged to the league and had equal voting representation, they did not surrender their autonomy or sovereignty. The tribes adopted this form of government and peace returned. One honorary seat was then set aside for Deganaweda.

When the English saw this type of leadership, they were elated. They—the English males—did not want to deal with women in power, and the leadership council was ideal as their point of contact and negotiation with the powerful league. At this time the Iroquois League controlled more than one million square miles of fur-trapping territory. What the English failed to see, however, was that the Iroquois League and its member tribes made up a strong matrilineal society. Women owned everything, and lineage and property passed through the women's clans. Additionally, a man went to live with the woman's family when they were married. And although there were 49 men on the Iroquois Grand Council, the clan matrons voted each of these men into office. When votes were to be taken by the council, it was the clan matrons who went back to the people and "caucused" with the tribal members to get a sense of how the tribe's representative on the council should vote. If a council member voted contrary to the direction of the tribal members, she could remove him from office. It was then up to the women of the tribe to vote a new representative into the grand council. The same was true in case of death; if a council member died in office, the women of the clan selected a replacement.

Another cultural misunderstanding was the work of the Iroquois men and women. English men often wrote about the drudgery forced upon the Iroquois women, explaining that they and their children were forced into the bean, squash, and cornfields. What the English failed to understand, however, was that it was the women who owned the fields, it was the women who decided when it was time to harvest the crops, and the time women and children spent together was a critical part of Iroquois training. The women sang and told stories about the league to the children and passed down the history and traditions from generation to generation.

The English also criticized the Iroquois male as being a man of leisure. They commented that the men were often seen sitting under trees and smoking their pipes while repairing hunting equipment or birch-bark canoes. Then they would go off on the rivers in the area, and not return for a considerable length of time while the women toiled in the fields.

At the time of contact with the English, the Iroquois League controlled all of the fur trapping from the Atlantic Ocean west to the Mississippi River, and from the Great Lakes south to the present-day states of North and South Carolina. Numerous rivers traversed this large area and could be portaged by the shallow birch-bark canoes without any difficulty. The Iroquois men used the river system to visit the tributary tribes that the Iroquois had conquered and received yearly tribute in the way of trade goods. Iroquois men were absent for extended periods of time, but they were carrying out the role of the male in their society. The men represented the clan matrons in their control of the Iroquois League. Clearly, the English had misunderstood the role of the male and female in the Iroquois League.

AN IMPORTANT ROLE AT WOUNDED KNEE

Much like the English's inability to recognize the importance of the role women played in Iroquois society, the participation of Indian women at the Wounded Knee occupation is often overlooked. If credit is not given to the Indian women who participated in the Wounded Knee occupation, one is guilty of repeating the old injustices of the past. The keys to any prolonged siege are planning, manpower, tenacity, and a long, reliable supply line. Of all of these, it is the supply line that supports the others, and this was one of the key roles Indian women had during the occupation. Once the occupation had begun and the GOONs, assisted by the federal government, had established roadblocks around the village of Wounded Knee, the lack of planning for a prolonged occupation became very evident. Food and ammunition were scarce. A convenience store and several private residences were located in the village of Wounded Knee. The convenience store (owned by two non-Indians) was quickly stripped bare of all necessities. It was after this that Indian women made an extremely important, but overlooked,

Women played a major role in helping those who occupied Wounded Knee maintain their strength during the standoff. Not only did women smuggle food and ammunition into the town, but they also served as guides to bring in reinforcements to buoy AIM's numbers.

contribution. Indian women became the conduit through which food and ammunition were smuggled into Wounded Knee. One woman, DeCora Boyer, six months pregnant at the time, crawled across the surrounding fields at night carrying food and ammunition. As she approached the village, Boyer had to crawl under barbed-wire fences while avoiding the GOON and FBI patrols.

In the same way, Indian women served as guides to bring in new Indian occupiers to reinforce AIM members. Boyer, Anna Mae Aquash, and other young Indian women also participated in digging and maintaining the eight bunkers from which the occupiers occasionally returned fire against the GOON squad and federal marshals. In her book *Lakota Woman*, Mary Brave Bird, who is also known as Mary Crow Dog, stated: "Our women played a major part at Wounded Knee. We had two or three pistol-packing mamas swaggering around with six-shooters dangling at their hips, taking their turns on the firing line, swapping lead with the feds."[24]

There can be no doubt that the Indian women were exploited once they decided to remain at Wounded Knee. The tasks of housekeeping, meal preparation, and laundry fell to the women. They had little voice in deciding whether to do those tasks. Many women saw this as the only way to support the men in the fight against the federal government. They were not in the public eye like AIM leaders such as Russell Means, Dennis Banks, or John Trudell. The women became participating members of AIM and the occupation through whatever small contributions they could make. In his autobiography, *Where White Men Fear to Tread*, Means stated:

> Most Indian women in those years, like Gladys [Bissonette] and Ellen [Moves Camp], were strong, and they were also innately wise. Taking the glory was not on their agenda. Understanding the female-male balance, they felt no need to be anointed publicly with leadership. They also knew that whoever was up front usually ended up getting shot at or going to prison, so their contributions were usually from behind the scenes, functioning as an information network of advisers and keeping everyone informed and motivated.[25]

Some women disagreed. Brave Bird described the conflicts between women inside the siege in her book *Lakota Woman*. She stated:

The AIM leaders are particularly sexist, never having learned our true Indian history where women voted and participated equally in all matters of tribal life. They have learned the white man's way of talking down to women and regarding their position as inferior. Some gave us the impression that we were there for their use and that we should be flattered to have their children.[26]

Perhaps Kenneth Stern best summed this up in his book *Loud Hawk, the United States versus the American Indian Movement.* Stern relates that Indian women did the best work in the early days of Indian activism, but once the Indian men came on the scene the women were pushed into the kitchen or out of the picture.[27] Eventually, Indian women, tired of being pushed into subservient roles, formed their own organization, Women of All Red Nations (WARN). WARN is not concerned with overt, aggressive activism but focuses instead on improving the lives of Indian people, raising awareness about AIDS and drugs, preventing Indian youth suicide, and stopping the proliferation of the dumping of solid and toxic waste on Indian reservations.

7

Trials, Prison, and the End of Red Power

WHEN THE OCCUPATION OF WOUNDED KNEE ENDED on May 8, 1973, two Indians were dead and an unknown number were wounded on both sides, including casualties among federal government forces. Many of the AIM members involved in the siege spent the years that followed in courtrooms, in hiding, or in prison as a result of their actions at Wounded Knee and the shoot-out at the Jumping Bull compound in 1975. According to American Indian Movement leader Dennis Banks, Wounded Knee was a mixed blessing:

> For AIM, the 71-day standoff with the FBI and U.S. marshals represented a high-water mark. It was a bold assertion of Indian sovereignty and resistance and it captured the nation's attention. But Wounded Knee and its violent aftermath would also lead to AIM's fragmentation and, in the view of critics, its moral collapse.[28]

After the occupation of Wounded Knee came to an end on May 8, 1973, several AIM members spent many years in court for the role they played in the conflict. Between 1974 and 1976, Russell Means, who is pictured here leaving the district court building in St. Paul, Minnesota, was tried on 12 different occasions for a variety of offenses.

AIM ACTIVISM

Other Red Power activism events that were carried out by AIM members, or grew out of the AIM militancy, included the six-month occupation of a former girls' camp on state-owned land at Moss Lake, New York; the five-week armed occupation of a vacant Alexian Brothers novitiate by the "Menominee Warrior Society" near the Menominee Reservation in Wisconsin; the eight-day takeover of a tribally owned Fairchild electronics assembly plant on the Navajo Reservation in New Mexico; a three-day occupation of the Yankton Sioux Industries plant on the reservation near Wagner, South Dakota; and a weeklong occupation of a juvenile detention center by members of the Puyallup tribe in Washington State.

It is important to understand that the American Indian Movement was made up of volunteer Red Power activists who were charismatic leaders and dedicated followers who sought redress against the federal government for wrongs committed against Indian nations and people. The American Indian Movement reached its height decades prior to the advent of Indian-owned casinos and the perception of "rich Indians." AIM operated on a budget of money donated from outside sources. Some tribal governments, but not many, were in a position to donate a few thousand dollars, but food, housing, and transportation costs far exceeded the resources. AIM leaders often turned to local churches and solicited donations, reminding the church leaders that they had failed to assist Indian nations while at the same time attempting to convert Indians into their particular denomination and encouraging the adoption of Indian children by non-Indian families. Some churches felt guilty and provided gifts of food and small amounts of money. AIM activists depended largely (almost totally) on the goodwill of other Indian people who took them into their homes, fed them, hid them, and provided gas money whenever possible.

WKLD/OC

In March 1973, 17 lawyers and legal workers from across the country established the Wounded Knee Legal Defense/Offense Committee (WKLD/OC) in Rapid City, South Dakota, to provide legal assistance for the trials that came out of the occupation. The committee's objectives were "to provide an adequate defense for those charged with crimes in or about Wounded Knee, to encourage the return of the rule of law to the area surrounding Wounded Knee, to permit residents to return to their homes, to prohibit federal agents from making further illegal arrests, and to make the facts about Wounded Knee known to the American public."

More than 400 people were arrested at Wounded Knee, resulting in 275 cases in federal, state, and tribal courts. The WKLD/OC represented all defendants in federal and tribal Wounded Knee cases. Seven defendants were charged with major conspiracy and 127 defendants faced charges of breaking and entering, larceny, conspiracy, and interfering with federal marshals. There were 97 persons charged and tried in the Oglala Sioux tribal courts for riot or unlawful assembly as defined in the tribal code. The WKLD/OC also handled cases arising from events both prior to and following

Leonard Peltier, who was convicted and sentenced to two consecutive life sentences for the murders of two FBI agents at Pine Ridge Reservation in 1975, has long been a symbol for Native American activists. Many groups, including Amnesty International, consider Peltier (who is depicted in this painting) a political prisoner, and believe he did not receive a fair trial.

the occupation, including protests at Scottsbluff, Nebraska, and Custer, Rapid City, and Sioux Falls, South Dakota.

The WKLD/OC was successful in obtaining a court ruling that stated it would not be possible for the Indian defendants to obtain a fair trial in South Dakota. The trials of the AIM leaders were moved to St. Paul, Minnesota, and Cedar Rapids, Iowa, while the remaining cases were moved to Lincoln, Nebraska; Council Bluffs, Iowa; Bismarck, North Dakota; and Sioux Falls, Aberdeen, and Rapid City, South Dakota. With the trial locations spread out, the WKLD/OC had to maintain a number of offices, thereby placing a heavy burden on the committee's resources. The WKLD/OC's reliance on volunteers resulted in a continual change in personnel that necessitated the establishment of strict office rules and internal security.

THE AMERICAN INDIAN MOVEMENT TODAY

The American Indian Movement no longer exists as a national organization, but that is not to say that AIM has totally disappeared from the scene as an Indian activist organization.

Following the Wounded Knee occupation and the incarceration of the AIM leaders, the national organization disintegrated. What emerged, however, were individual state chapters of AIM. Those still exist today. They have no central leadership or charter, and are not affiliated with each other. They attempt to raise concerns over the federal government's continued failure to meet the needs of Indian people. In 2004, for example, they protested the bicentennial of the Lewis and Clark expedition and even threatened to blow up the keel boat used by the reenactment group in Pierre, South Dakota. However, the group is a mere shadow of its former self, providing a limited voice to a small number of activists.

Security became a major concern as the trials progressed and the presence of government COUNTERINTELPRO informants became known. Prior to her murder, Anna Mae Aquash worked and lived in the Rapid City WKLD/OC office, and it was at that time that the suspicion first emerged that she was possibly an FBI informant.

Many of the difficulties the WKLD/OC faced were financial and were the direct result of the tenacity with which the U.S. government pursued the Wounded Knee cases. The WKLD/OC and the defendants argued that the government's objective in bringing such a large number of cases to court was to use the indictments and the court system to financially destroy AIM and the Red Power activism it fostered among Indian people. They were correct. The acquittal and dismissal rate was a bittersweet victory. Funds for the WKLD/OC trickled to a halt before all of the cases against the Indian defendants could be adjudicated. AIM leaders were by that time in prison or in hiding in the United States or Canada. They had failed to develop a funding base, but more importantly, the AIM leadership became caught up in the media frenzy surrounding the ordeal and did not seek out and train a new generation of activists that could resurrect AIM and reinvigorate the Red Power movement. "Red Power" is now more a slogan than a driving force, as relatively few Indian people are aware of the widespread activism of the 1960s and 1970s. Leonard Peltier is now confined in the U.S. Penitentiary in Terre Haute, Indiana, serving two life sentences for the murders of Ronald Williams and Jack Coler during the Jumping Bull FBI raid in 1975. Aquash's murderers may or may not be convicted. AIM as it was in the 1970s is dead as well: killed by the FBI and bankrupted by the state and federal court systems.

The Legacy of Red Power and Wounded Knee

RED POWER ACTIVISM CONTINUED TO INFLUENCE U.S. governmental officials until late in the twentieth century and into the beginning of the twenty-first. On October 21, 1996, President Bill Clinton reaffirmed the federal government's commitment to educating Indian people.

> There is in America, across the lines of race and class and region, a profound concern for our children. Too many are poor or sick or unsupervised. Too many are likely to use violence or be the victims of violence. Too many are unprepared intellectually for life or work. Yet nothing is so striking in tribal communities as your love of family and extended family and your devotion to your children. Every segment of our society could well take a lesson from you. But in spite of your best efforts, too many of your children also suffer from poor health and inadequate education. And we are trying hard to address these problems. You mentioned Head Start; our budget calls for continued, substantial increases and expansions of the Head Start

program, as well as the Women and Infants and Children program.

Our education plan, called Goals 2000, for the first time sets world-class education standards for every school and all our children and gives local communities the grass-roots support they need to achieve those goals. Goals 2000 contains millions more next year for BIA-funded schools and schools serving Native Alaskans. And these funds cannot be spent until the education goals of your community are considered.[29]

THE IMPORTANCE OF EDUCATION

John Echohawk, a Pawnee Indian and the executive director of the Native American Rights Fund, summed up the importance of education to Indian people and Indian tribes today in an article in *Children Today*:

> The importance of education for Native youth and their Tribes has taken on new dimensions in this modern era of Indian self-determination, in which Indian Tribes have taken their rightful place among the councils of governments in this country. Tribal governments are becoming increasingly sophisticated and are involved in a growing range of governmental functions, including taxation and environmental regulation.
>
> To properly carry out these responsibilities and programs, tribal governments need trained, educated Indian people who can perform the Tribal jobs and do them in ways that respect and integrate Tribal tradition and culture. College educated Indians have increasingly filled those jobs for Tribal governments, but more college educated youths are needed as the challenges grow. . . . There was a time when people thought that Indians could not be educated or did not want to be educated. As more and more Indians graduate from college today, that myth is destroyed.[30]

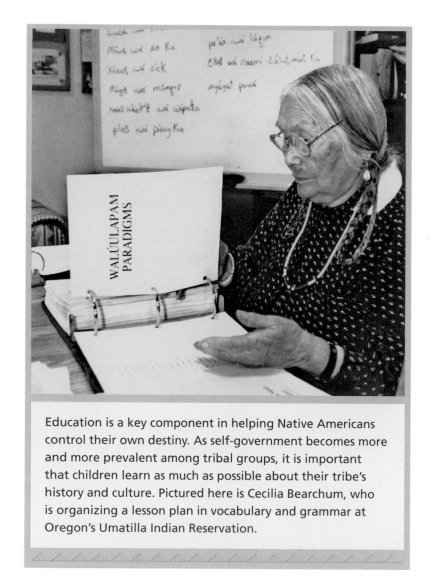

Education is a key component in helping Native Americans control their own destiny. As self-government becomes more and more prevalent among tribal groups, it is important that children learn as much as possible about their tribe's history and culture. Pictured here is Cecilia Bearchum, who is organizing a lesson plan in vocabulary and grammar at Oregon's Umatilla Indian Reservation.

Echohawk's call for education for Indian people was actualized in 1978, when Congress passed Public Law 95-471, the Tribally Controlled Community College Assistance Act. Red Power activists were in the forefront of the call for these culturally relevant educational institutions. Studies conducted by the federal government that surveyed Indian educational progress indicated that many Indian youths felt culturally alienated in mainstream public and private college institutions. The limited number of Indian students graduating from high school and college inspired Congress to allow tribal communities to exercise full autonomy concerning education on their reservations.

Indian students were tired of going into college classrooms where American Indian history was taught by non-Indian professors who still spoke of the "tawny savages" having been defeated and eliminated as a people in 1890. Young Red Power activists, many of whom were involved in the Wounded Knee occupation, began to demand courses that were relevant to Indian people.

Most tribal colleges established under the authority of the 1978 act fulfilled these demands. They are physically and culturally unique, offering curricula based on the needs of their tribal youth. The colleges vary in size, facilities, course offerings, and degrees and certificates offered. Most tribal colleges place extraordinary emphasis on student retention and success. In Indian country, academic success, physical well-being, and personal esteem are inseparable. What happens at home and in the community eventually translates to performance in the classroom. With this in mind, unique personal and academic perspectives are therefore promoted throughout the campuses. In addition to traditional academic courses, the tribal colleges also offer a wide range of vocational courses in response to specific tribal economic needs. They also provide academic programs that prepare students to transfer to four-year colleges, such as Sinte Gleska College located on the Rosebud Sioux Reservation in South Dakota.

It is important to emphasize that the success of tribal colleges rests on an Indian cultural foundation as reflected in the Red Power movement. Equally important is the recognition that the future of Indian tribes rests on the education of their youth. Ron McNeil, a Hunkpapa Lakota and president of the American Indian College Fund, stated:

As more and more Native American children decide to attend college, the number of tribal colleges in the United States will continue to grow. Today, there are 32 tribal colleges in 12 states that serve approximately 30,000 students. Pictured here is Sitting Bull Community College president Ron His Horse Is Thunder during the groundbreaking ceremony of the new campus in Fort Yates, North Dakota, in 2003.

As a descendant of Sitting Bull and as an educator, I am committed to doing all I can to lighten the burden of poverty by supporting those grassroots institutions that are bringing about change. I believe the growing band of 29 American Indian colleges are absolutely crucial to the survival and growth of our Native American communities. In spite of the harsh statistics, there is great wisdom and courage in Indian country. Their survival is so important that I cannot just sit by. . . . The most important thing tribal colleges offer to Indian communities is hope. They are bringing new life to the reservations in the form of education and training.[31]

A CHANGE IN GOVERNMENT POLICY

There can be little doubt that the Red Power movement had a profound and positive impact on U.S. government policy toward Indian nations. The oft-spoken goal of the activists was one of self-determination for Indian people—the rights of Indians to handle their own affairs with as little government intervention as possible. Clyde Warrior, a Ponca Indian and cofounder of the National Indian Youth Council (NIYC), explained the powerlessness and lack of self-determination to government officials in Washington, D.C., in 1967:

> We are not allowed to make those basic human choices and decisions about our personal life and about the destiny of our communities, which is the mark of free mature people. We sit on our front porch or in our yards, and the world and our lives in it pass us by without our desires or aspiration having any effect.[32]

In a sense, Indian self-determination was an offshoot of the government policy of termination of Indian tribes and tribal people. A new series of federal Indian policies were initiated in post–World War II America that were intended to terminate the special status of Indian tribes and to assimilate Indian people into mainstream American society. Under the termination policy, the treaty relationship and trust responsibility between the federal government and Indian people would come to an end. Indian people would be relocated to urban areas, where they were expected to melt into the dominant society. What happened, in fact, was just the opposite. The termination era, generally assigned the dates of 1945 to 1961, was a failure. The federal programs were poorly thought out, underfunded, and ultimately failed. American Indians in urban areas were forgotten, neglected, and angry. The occupation of Wounded Knee reflected that anger, and the change in government polices toward Indian people reflected the impact of that occupation and specifically the impact of Red Power.

On January 4, 1975, Congress passed Public Law 93-638, the Indian Self-Determination and Education Assistance Act, which expanded tribal control over tribal governments and education. The act also encouraged the development of human resources and reservation programs and authorized federal funds to build needed public school facilities on or near Indian reservations. The act was hailed by many as the most important piece of legislation passed since the 1934 Indian Reorganization Act. The ultimate goal of the Self-Determination Act was to give governing authority (self-determination) over federal programs to the tribes and to end programs that promoted federal dependency and paternalism. Pursuant to a joint resolution of both houses, Congress agreed to review the government's historical and special legal relationship with Indian people.

In April 1978, Congress passed the American Indian Religious Freedom Act (AIRFA) to recognize, protect, and preserve the inherent right of American Indians to express and exercise their traditions and beliefs. AIRFA clarified U.S. policy pertaining to the protection of Native Americans' religious freedom and acknowledged that the special nature of Indian religions had frequently resulted in conflicts between federal laws and policies and religious freedom. AIRFA recognized also that some federal laws, such as those protecting wilderness areas or endangered species, had inadvertently given rise to problems such as denial of access to sacred sites or prohibitions on the possession of animal-derived sacred objects by Native Americans. The AIFRA stated:

It shall be the policy of the United States to protect and preserve for Indians their inherent right of freedom to believe, express, and exercise the traditional religions of the American Indian, Eskimo, Aleut, and Native Hawaiians, including but not limited to access to sites, use and possession of sacred objects, and the freedom to worship through ceremonials and traditional rites.[33]

THE IMPORTANCE OF PRESERVING ONE'S IDENTITY

By the mid-1970s American Indian people had begun to express their concerns regarding the placement of Indian children in non-Indian foster and adoptive homes. These concerns included a disproportionately large number of Indian children who were being removed from their birth families; the frequency with which these children were placed in non-Indian substitute care and adoptive settings; the failure of public agencies to consider legitimate cultural differences when dealing with Indian families; and the documented lack of service to the Indian population. Indian tribes, mental health professionals, and legal advocates reported that between 25 and 35 percent of Indian children were annually placed outside natural tribal and family environments. Research indicated that these children suffered extraordinary trauma. American Indian children placed in non-Indian homes for adoptive or foster care suffered a rate of 70 suicides per 100,000, six times the rate of the general youth population in the United States. In 1987, Dr. Irving N. Berlin reported, "There are considerable data to indicate that the more than 50,000 American Indian children adoptees in Anglo homes are at considerable risk." Berlin continued:

> One of the factors, a part of being Indian, is the richness of the history, richness of the traditions, of extended families. For example, a child [if removed] would miss out on the different legends and stories, which their grandfather might tell them, or they'd miss out on helping their

grandmother, do different activities with their family, and in the community. They would miss out on all the beautiful things about being a Native, all the richness and diversity of their culture. They would miss out on their language. The most important concern for our children is the development of a good self-esteem. We feel that with good self-esteem a Native child can succeed and do anything that they want anywhere that they want—but they've got to have a good grounding. In order to have a good grounding, it is essential that they stay within the Native community where people love them and care for them and are able to give them that extra richness.[34]

To address these concerns, in November 1978, Congress passed the Indian Child Welfare Act (ICWA). The ICWA removed sole authority for the protection of Indian children and the delivery of child welfare services from the individual states; reestablished tribal authority to accept or reject jurisdiction over Indian children not living on reservations; and required state courts and public child welfare agencies to follow specific legal and procedural requirements when considering foster or adoptive placement of Indian children.

IGRA

On October 17, 1988, in keeping with the Red Power movement's call for Indian self-determination, Congress passed a watershed piece of legislation that had far-reaching consequences for Indian and non-Indian people: the Indian Gaming Regulatory Act (IGRA). The IGRA was designed "to establish federal standards and regulations for conducting gaming activities within Indian country as a means of promoting tribal economic development, self-sufficiency, and strong tribal governments."[35]

The IGRA was enacted because of concerns expressed by non-Indian reservation neighbors, federal officials, and some tribal officials. Indian gaming, it appeared, was growing rapidly, but without any controlling structure or regulation. Many states objected to what they considered to be a proliferation of "Indian Casinos," voicing a fear of increased gambling addiction and infiltration by organized crime and other corrupting influences. The IGRA was created and written to mitigate those fears. The IGRA provided for the establishment of federal regulations and federal standards regarding the conduct of gaming on Indian lands. To ensure the effective regulation of gaming operations, the IGRA established the National Indian Gaming Commission, which has the authority to monitor gaming on Indian lands.

In 1988, Congress passed the Indian Gaming Regulatory Act, which permitted gaming on Indian reservations. Pictured here is Foxwoods Resort Casino on the Mashantucket Pequot Reservation in Ledyard, Connecticut. The casino is the largest in the world and has nearly 400 gaming tables and more than 7,000 slot machines.

Following passage of the IGRA, Indian nations whose reservations (once thought to be worthless land) were located in close proximity to American urban centers began to develop elaborate and sophisticated gaming facilities. These

NONFEDERALLY RECOGNIZED TRIBES

The Indian Gaming and Regulatory Act applies only to federally recognized Indian tribes. There are more than 100 Indian tribes that are not federally recognized. They have this status because they were considered to no longer exist after the colonial wars of the 1500s to 1700s, the Indian wars of the American Revolution period, the Indian Removal of the 1830s and 1840s, and the Great Plains warfare of the mid to late 1800s. Equally or more destructive was Public Law 280, which beginning in 1953, put into motion a series of congressional treaty abrogations and termination of Indian reservations.

The people of these tribes were still Indians, but the federal government no longer recognized them as such. In California, government treaty parties negotiated 19 treaties with Indian nations in the mid-1800s, all of which signed away their lands. Congress never ratified the treaties; however, it did take the land from the residents. The Indian people of those tribes became nonfederally recognized. As a result, today there are thousands of full-blood Indian people in California who are not recognized by the federal government of the United States.

When the state of California negotiated the Indian Gaming and Regulatory Act agreements with the federally recognized tribes to authorize gaming, a provision was added that calls for a percentage of the gross income from gaming be set aside and distributed annually to the members of nonfederally recognized tribes. This is done the first working day of January each year and distributes millions of dollars to the people who were robbed of their lands.

casinos were often designed and built by the same companies that built the Reno, Atlantic City, and Las Vegas gambling facilities.

NAGPRA

For centuries, American Indian people have shown increasing concern and unrest over the desecration of native burial grounds, looting of ancient Indian gravesites, and the inhumane collection of Native American skeletal remains and related sacred (funerary) objects. Although anthropologists argued that there was "much to be learned" from the study of Indian human remains, Indian scholars pointed out that skeletal remains had been held against Indian wishes since the late 1800s and that little if any research had taken place. To claim, as many anthropologists did in the late 1900s, that they were now ready to "study Indian bones" was an unconscionable excuse to protect museum and university collections. Once again, American Indians, many of whom had participated in the occupations of Alcatraz Island and Wounded Knee, turned to Congress for recognition of their tribal sovereignty and the self-determination to control their cultural heritage and preserve the dignity of who they are as native people. In 1990, Congress responded to years of lobbying and pressure from Indian tribes and passed into law the Native American Graves Protection and Repatriation Act (NAGPRA). The act protected Native American burial sites and the removal of human remains, funerary objects, sacred objects, and objects of cultural patrimony on federal, Indian, and Native Hawaiian lands. The act also set up a process by which federal agencies and museums receiving federal funds are required to inventory holdings of such remains and objects and work with appropriate Indian tribes and Native Hawaiian organizations to reach agreement on repatriation or other disposition of these remains and objects.

SELF-GOVERNANCE

Perhaps the most exciting outcome of Red Power and Wounded Knee, as it relates to Indian people, and certainly in keeping with the twin goals of tribal sovereignty and self-determination, was the passage into law of the Tribal Self-Governance Act. On July 2 and 3, 1990, Assistant Secretary of the Interior Eddie Brown signed historic agreements with six tribes: the Quinault Indian Nation, Tahola, Washington; Lummi Indian Nation, Bellingham, Washington; Jamestown Klallam Indian tribe, Sequim, Washington; Hoopa Valley Indian tribe, Hoopa, California; Cherokee Nation, Tahlequah, Oklahoma; and the Mille Lacs band of Chippewa Indians, Onamia, Minnesota. These tribes were part of a self-governance pilot program that would ultimately give up to 20 tribes the authority to administer and set priorities for federal funds received directly from the government and bypass the control of the Bureau of Indian Affairs (BIA). On December 4, 1991, Congress passed legislation to amend the Indian Self-Determination and Education Assistance Act. Entitled the Tribal Self-Governance Demonstration Project, the act extended the number of tribes taking part in the tribal self-governance pilot project from 20 to 30.

The principles guiding the initial negotiation of these compacts, originally defined by Indian leaders in 1986 and 1987, emphasized the establishment of a government-to-government relationship with the United States on a tribe-by-tribe basis. Emphasis was placed on the importance of these agreements being negotiated between each Indian government and the U.S. government as a whole, instead of Indian governments dealing with individual governmental agencies.

Thirty-three Native American nations concluded one or more compacts of self-government with the United States between 1990 and 1995. Three studies were conducted in

1993, 1994, and 1995 to provide annual self-governance assessments. The first study in 1993 emphasized Indian government compliance with compacts and the effectiveness of accounting and budgetary systems. The second and third studies conducted focused on "costs and benefit," in order to ascertain compliance by Indian governments and officials of the BIA and the Office of Self-Governance.

The annual studies generally approved the creative and effective activities of Indian governments but were critical of the U.S. government's compliance with congressional and compact terms and requirements. The Center for World Indigenous Studies released the final report of the Self-Government Process Evaluation on July 1, 1996. The report stated in part that "based on a review of documents [historical and contemporary] that . . . the United States government generally is not seriously participating in the development and conduct of the self-government initiative." The report was encouraging for Native American nations, however, and stated that, "Baseline Measures Reports from subject Indian governments and the study conducted by the Department of the Interior [August 1995] confirms that Indian governments have made major progress toward social and economic development as a direct result of the self-governance initiative."

Consequently, Indian governments have, in very large part, Red Power activists to thank for their efforts over two decades to promote self-government and restoration of Native Americans' rights. Red Power activists brought the U.S. government policies of termination and relocation to an end, and as a result, Indian nations have entered into an era of self-governance and are now recognized as sovereign nations.

Chronology

1492 Genoan explorer Christopher Columbus, sailing under a Spanish flag, encounters the indigenenous peoples of the Caribbean and sets into motion the largest genocide the world has ever known; in the Caribbean and Mesoamerica, more than 60 million Indian people die of diseases of European origin, warfare, or are literally worked to death; in the present-day United States, the Indian population is reduced from

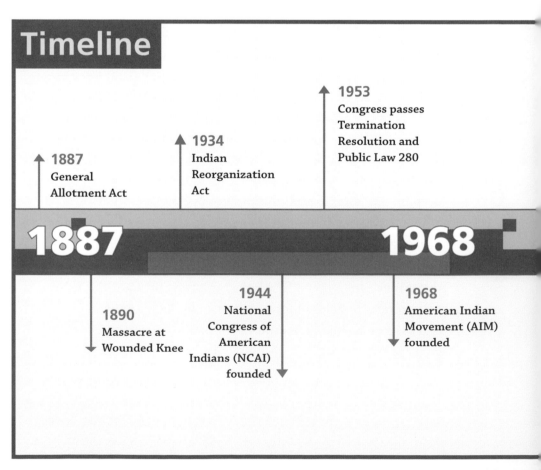

Timeline

1887
General Allotment Act

1934
Indian Reorganization Act

1953
Congress passes Termination Resolution and Public Law 280

1887   **1968**

1890
Massacre at Wounded Knee

1944
National Congress of American Indians (NCAI) founded

1968
American Indian Movement (AIM) founded

approximately 10 million at the time of
European contact to a nadir of about 25,000
in 1890. Thus begins the timeline
of American Indian activism.

1887 Congress passes the General Allotment Act.

1890 Massacre at Wounded Knee; estimates
of deaths are as high as 300 Indian men,
women, and children.

1934 Congress passes the Indian Reorganization
Act.

1944 National Congress of American Indians
(NCAI) founded.

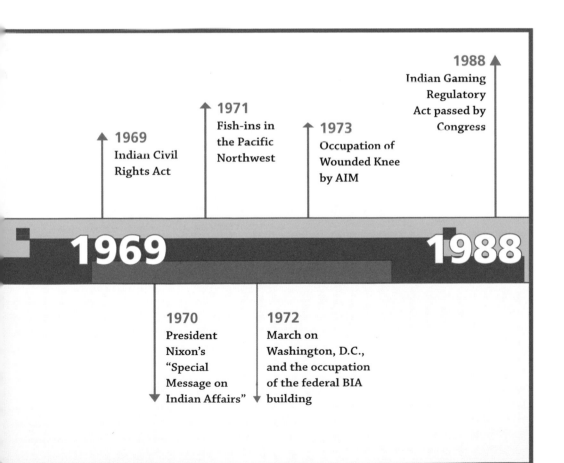

1969
Indian Civil
Rights Act

1971
Fish-ins in
the Pacific
Northwest

1973
Occupation of
Wounded Knee
by AIM

1988
Indian Gaming
Regulatory
Act passed by
Congress

1969

1988

1970
President
Nixon's
"Special
Message on
Indian Affairs"

1972
March on
Washington, D.C.,
and the occupation
of the federal BIA
building

1953   Congress passes Termination Resolution and Public Law 280.

1961   National Indian Youth Council (NIYC) founded.

1968   American Indian Movement (AIM) founded by Clyde Bellecourt, Eddie Benton Banai, Dennis Banks, and Mary Jane Wilson.

1969   Occupation of Alcatraz Island by American Indian college students; passage of Indian Civil Rights Act.

1970   President Richard Nixon's "Special Message on Indian Affairs"; Nixon denounces past federal policies, pronounces the end of termination, and calls for a new era of self-determination for Indian people; occupation of Mount Rushmore by AIM; Native American Rights Fund (NARF) established.

1970–1971   A group of Indian and Chicano activists begin discussions with the federal government on acquiring 650 acres of land that was formerly a Strategic Air Command military base but now will be used for an American Indian college; November 1970: when it appears that the land will not be granted, 40 American Indians occupy the site; on April 1, 1971, the federal government formally turns over the title, and with funds from the Ford Foundation and federal grants, classes begin on July 7, 1971, at what becomes known as Deganawide-Quetzalcoatl University.

1971   United Native Americans occupy bungalow at University of California, Berkeley, and later receive permission to develop a Native American cultural center; center developed into one of the first American Indian studies centers in the nation.

Young Indian activists adopt some of the ideas and tactics of the civil rights movement and hold numerous fish-ins in the Pacific Northwest.

1972 The idea for the Trail of Broken Treaties, the march on Washington, D.C., and the occupation of the federal BIA building; occupation ends on November 8, 1972; Indian Education Act.

1973 Occupation of Wounded Knee, led by the American Indian Movement; occupation lasts for 71 days.

1975 Indian Self-Determination and Education Assistance Act passed by Congress.

1988 Indian Gaming Regulatory Act passed by Congress.

Notes

Chapter 1

1. The "Requiremento," which had been framed by the famous jurist Palacias Rubios, was normally read in Spanish to the trees, or mumbled by the attacking army.
2. *Johnson v. McIntosh*, 21 U.S. 543, 5 L.Ed. 681, 8 Wheat. 543 (1823) March 10, 1823.
3. *Cherokee Nation v. State of Georgia*, 30 U.S. 1 (1831). 30 U.S. 1 (Pet.).
4. *Samuel A. Worcester v. State of Georgia*. 31 U.S. 515; 8 L. Ed. 483; 1832.

Chapter 2

5. John G. Neihardt, *Black Elk Speaks* (Lincoln and London: University of Nebraska Press, 1995), 207.
6. A Massacre Survivor Speaks: Available online at *http://www.dickshovel.com/DwyBrd.html*.
7. Ibid.

Chapter 3

8. Walter Wetzel, former president of the National Congress of American Indians. Quoted in Stan Steiner, *The New Indians* (New York: Harper and Row, 1968), 45.
9. Wallace "Mad Bear" Anderson, Quoted in *The New Indians*, 282.
10. Vine Deloria Jr., *Behind the Trail of Broken Treaties: An Indian Declaration of Independence* (Austin: University of Texas Press, 1985), 34.
11. Melvin Thom, President of the NIYC, Quoted in *The New Indians*, 43.
12. *The Warpath*, San Francisco, Calif., 1968, Quoted in Jack Forbes, *Native Americans and Nixon* (Los Angeles: American Indian Studies Center, 1981), 28.
13. President Lyndon Baynes Johnson, Speech before U.S. Senate, 1970.
14. The Reverend Tony Calaman, Public Forum before the Committee on Urban Indians in San Francisco, April 1969.
15. LaDonna Harris, National Council on Indian Opportunity (NCIO, Public Forum before the Committee on Urban Indians in San Francisco, April 1969.
16. Richard McKenzie, Meeting at the San Francisco Indian Center, 1969.
17. President Richard Nixon, Speech before the delegates of the NCAI gathered in Omaha, Nebraska, September, 1968.
18. Ibid.

Chapter 4

19. Russell Means in W. Dale Mason's, "You Can Only Kick So Long: AIM leadership in Nebraska, 1972–79," *Journal of the West*, 1984.

20. Robert Robideau in Nora Antoinette, *Who Would Unbraid Her Hair: The Legend of Annie Mae* (Ashland, Ore.: Anam Cara Press, 1999), 257.

21. U.S. Department of Justice, Accounting For Native American Deaths, Pine Ridge Indian Reservation South Dakota, May 2000.

Chapter 5

22. Carter Camp, "War Stories and Wounded Knee: 1973." Available online at *http://www. freepeltier.org/031404_war_ stories_wk73.htm.*

Chapter 6

23. Dr. Elizabeth Castle, unpublished manuscript, "Women Were the Backbone Men Were the Jawbone" of the American Indian Movement.

24. Brave Bird, quoted in Crow Dog, *Lakota Woman* (New York: Harper Perennial, 1991), 191–92.

25. Russell Means, *Where White Men Fear to Tread* (New York: St. Martin's Griffin, 1995), 255–65.

26. Brave Bird, quoted in Crow Dog, *Lakota Woman* (New York: Harper Perennial, 1991), 68–69.

27. Kenneth Stern, *Loud Hawk, the United States versus the American Indian Movement* (Norman: University of Oklahoma Press, 1994), 112.

Chapter 7

28. Vine Deloria Jr., *American Indian Policy in the Twentieth Century* (Norman: University of Oklahoma, 1992), 112.

Chapter 8

29. President William Jefferson Clinton, U.S. State DEPT. DISPATCH, Volume 7, Number 43, October 21, 1996.

30. John Echohawk, *Children Today* (Washington, D.C.: U.S. Government Printing Office, 1977), 12–13.

31. Ron McNeil, Sitting Bull College. Standing Rock Indian Reservation. 1996.

32. Clyde Warrior Address to the Native American Youth Council. Washington, D.C. 1967.

33. American Indian Religious Freedom Act, 1978.

34. "Adults Who Were Foster Children," in Troy R. Johnson, *The Indian Child Welfare Act: Indian Homes for Indian Children* (Los Angeles: University of California, 1990), 208–09.

35. The Indian Gaming Regulatory Act (IGRA), Public Law 100-497.

Bibliography

Alaska Native Claims Settlement Act, Public Law 92-203. Congress, session. December 18, 1971.

Ambler, Marjane. *Breaking the Iron Bonds: Indian Control of Energy Development.* Lawrence: University Press of Kansas, 1990.

Apess, William. "Eulogy on King Philip." Boston, 1836. Reprinted in James G. Abourezk. "Papers 1970–1983: Wounded Knee, 1973." The University of South Dakota. Available online at *http://www.usd.edu/library/special/wk73hist.htm.* Accessed December 28, 2006.

Clinton, William J. "Remarks to American Indian and Alaska Native Tribal Leaders." *The American Presidency Project*, 1994.

Congressional Research Service, CRS Issue Brief, "Gambling on Indian Reservations," January 2, 1989.

Cornell, Stephen. *The Return of the Native: American Indian Political Resurgence.* New York: Oxford University Press, 1988.

Deloria, Vine Jr. *American Indian Policy in the Twentieth Century.* Norman: University of Oklahoma Press, 1992.

El Nasser, Haya. "Critics Want Reservation Gaming Curbs." *USA Today*, May 20, 1993.

Getches, David H., Charles F. Wilkinson, and Robert A. Williams Jr. *Cases and Materials on Federal Indian Law,* 4th ed. American Casebook Series. St. Paul, Minn.: West Group, 1998.

Gordon-McCutchan, R. C. *The Taos Indians and the Battle for Blue Lake.* Sante Fe, N.M.: Red Crane Books, 1991.

Nagel, Joane. *American Indian Ethnic Renewal: Red Power and the Resurgence of Identity and Culture.* New York: Oxford University Press, 1996.

Nuclear Waste Policy Act of 1982, Public Law 97-425. Congress, session. January 7, 1983.

Public Law 100-497, Appendix A. Congress, session. February 25, 1987.

Reagan, Ronald. *American Indian Policy Statement, Public Papers of the Presidents of the United States.* Book 1, January 1 to July 1, 1983. Washington, D.C.: Unites States Government Printing Office, 1984.

Ryser, Rudolph C. *Indian Self-Government Process Evaluation Project, Preliminary Findings.* Olympia, Wash.: Center for World Indigenous Studies, 1995.

Senese, Guy B. *Self-Determination and the Social Education of Native Americans.* New York: Praeger, 1991.

Taos Indians, Blue Lake Bill, Public Law 91-550. Congress, session. December 15, 1970.

"Tribal Leaders Want Gaming Bill Withdrawn," *American Indian Report* 10, no. 8 (August 1994).

Further Reading

Abourezk, James G. "Papers 1970–1983: Wounded Knee, 1973." The University of South Dakota. Available online at *http://www.usd.edu/library/special/wk73hist.htm*. Accessed December 28, 2006.

Cornell, Stephen. *The Return of the Native: American Indian Political Resurgence*. New York: Oxford University Press, 1988.

Deloria, Vine Jr. *American Indian Policy in the Twentieth Century*. Norman: University of Oklahoma Press, 1992.

Getches, David H., Charles F. Wilkinson, and Robert A. Williams Jr. *Cases and Materials on Federal Indian Law,* 4th ed. American Casebook Series. St. Paul, Minn.: West Group, 1998.

Gordon-McCutchan, R. C. *The Taos Indians and the Battle for Blue Lake*. Sante Fe, N.M.: Red Crane Books, 1991.

Grossman, Mark. *The ABC-CLIO Companion to the Native American Rights Movement*. Santa Barbara, Calif: ABC-CLIO, 1996.

Johnson, Troy. *The Occupation of Alcatraz Island: Indian Self-Determination & The Rise of Indian Activism*. Urbana: University of Illinois Press, 1996.

———, Joane Nagel, and Duane Champagne. *American Indian Activism: Alcatraz to the Longest Walk*. Urbana: University of Illinois Press, 1997.

Matthiessen, Peter. *In the Spirit of Crazy Horse*. New York: Penguin Books, 1992.

Nagel, Joane. *American Indian Ethnic Renewal: Red Power and the Resurgence of Identity and Culture*. New York: Oxford University Press, 1996.

Smith, Paul C., and Robert Allen Warrior. *Like A Hurricane: The Indian Movement from Alcatraz to Wounded Knee*. New York: The New Press, 1996.

WEB SITES

AIM and Wounded Knee Documents
http://www.aics.org/WK/index.html

American Indian Movement
http://www.aimovement.org/

The Legacy of Wounded Knee
**http://www.argusleader.com/specialsections/2003/
woundedknee/**

Alcatraz: Occupation by the American Indian Movement
http://siouxme.com/lodge/alcatraz_np.html

James G. Abourezk, Papers 1970–1983
http://www.usd.edu/library/special/wk73hist.htm

Picture Credits

Index

About the Contributors

Author **TROY R. JOHNSON** is chair of the American Indian Studies program and Department of Anthropology at California State University, Long Beach. He is an internationally published scholar and is the author, editor, or associate editor of 16 books and numerous scholarly journal articles. His publications include *Distinguished Native American Spiritual Practitioners and Healers*; *The Occupation of Alcatraz Island: Indian Self-determination and the Rise of Indian Activism*; and *American Indian Activism, Alcatraz to The Longest Walk*. His areas of expertise also include American Indian activism, federal Indian law, Indian child welfare, and Indian youth suicide.

Series editor **PAUL C. ROSIER** received his Ph.D. in American history from the University of Rochester in 1998. Dr. Rosier currently serves as assistant professor of history at Villanova University, where he teaches Native American history, the environmental history of America, history of American Capitalism, and world history. He is the author of *Rebirth of the Blackfeet Nation, 1912–1954* (2001) and *Native American Issues* (2003). His next book, on post-World War II Native American politics, will be published in 2008 by Harvard University Press. Dr. Rosier's work has also appeared in various journals, including the *Journal of American History*, the *American Indian Culture and Research Journal*, and the *Journal of American Ethnic History*.